FastCourse Word 2007: Level 1

Jill Murphy
ExecuTrain of San Francisco

LABYRINTH
L E A R N I N G ®

FastCourse Word 2007: Level 1
by Jill Murphy

Copyright © 2009 by Labyrinth Learning

LABYRINTH
L E A R N I N G ®

Labyrinth Learning
PO Box 20818
El Sobrante, California 94820
800.522.9746
On the web at www.lablearning.com

President:
Brian Favro

Series Editor:
Russel Stolins

Acquisitions Editor:
Jason Favro

Managing Editor:
Laura A. Lionello

Production Manager:
Rad Proctor

Editorial/Production Team:
Amy Berk, Holly Hammond, Karen Henry,
ICC Macmillan, and Joyce S. Kaye

Indexing: Joanne Sprott

Cover Illustration:
Béatrice Favereau

Cover Design:
Seventeenth Street Studios

ITEM: 1-59136-200-8
ISBN-13: 978-1-59136-200-5

Manufactured in the United States of America.

10 9 8 7 6 5 4 3 2 1

FastCourse Word 2007: Level 1

Table of Contents

LESSON 4 CREATING A SIMPLE REPORT 60

LESSON 5 USING MAIL MERGE 84

LESSON 1

Working with Word Basics

In this lesson, you will get an overview of Microsoft Office Word 2007. First you will learn to start Word, and then how to work with the Word interface. You will open and close documents, navigate through a multipage document, and work with Word Help. Finally, you will exit the Word program.

LESSON OBJECTIVES

After studying this lesson, you will be able to:

- Work with the Microsoft Word 2007 Ribbon interface
- Use the Quick Access toolbar and the Mini toolbar
- Open and close documents
- Navigate in a document
- Use Word Help

LESSON TIMING

- Concepts/Hands-On:
  1 hr 00 min
- Concepts Review:
  15 min
- Total:
  1 hr 15 min

CASE STUDY: GETTING ORIENTED TO WORD 2007

Marissa Santos is studying to be a physician's assistant. In addition to her medical classes, she wants to take advantage of this opportunity to learn Microsoft Office Word 2007, so she can use it as a tool for working with her patients. She knows she'll need to use Word to take patient histories, maintain patient records, and so forth. She is currently researching diabetes for her nutrition class, and Word makes writing her research paper a snap.

Presenting Word 2007

Microsoft Office Word 2007 is a dynamic document-authoring program that lets you create and easily modify a variety of documents. Word provides tools to assist you in virtually every aspect of document creation. From desktop publishing to web publishing, Word has the right tool for the job. For these and many other reasons, Word is the most widely used word processing program in homes and businesses.

Starting Word

The method you use to start Word depends on whether you intend to create a new document or open an existing one. If you intend to create a new document, use one of the following methods to start Word:

- Click the ◆ start button, choose Microsoft Office from the All Programs menu, and then choose Microsoft Office Word 2007.

- Click the Microsoft Word 2007 ⓦ button on the quick launch toolbar located at the left edge of the taskbar. (This button may not appear on all computers.)

Use one of the following methods if you intend to open an existing Word document. Once the Word program starts, the desired document will open in a Word window.

- Navigate to the desired document using Windows Explorer or My Computer and double-click the document name.

- Click the ◆ start button and point to My Recent Documents. You can choose the desired document from the documents list, which displays the most recently used documents.

 Hands-On 1.1   **Start Word**

1. If necessary, start your computer. The Windows Desktop appears.

2. Click the ◆ start button at the left edge of the taskbar, and choose All Programs, just above the Start button.

3. Choose Microsoft Office→Microsoft Office Word 2007 from the menu.

4. Make sure the Word window is maximized ☐.

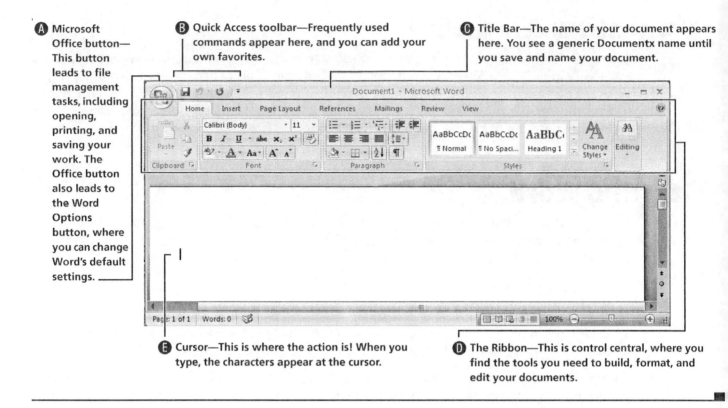

A Microsoft Office button—This button leads to file management tasks, including opening, printing, and saving your work. The Office button also leads to the Word Options button, where you can change Word's default settings.

B Quick Access toolbar—Frequently used commands appear here, and you can add your own favorites.

C Title Bar—The name of your document appears here. You see a generic Documentx name until you save and name your document.

E Cursor—This is where the action is! When you type, the characters appear at the cursor.

D The Ribbon—This is control central, where you find the tools you need to build, format, and edit your documents.

Opening Documents

The Open command on the Office menu displays the Open dialog box, where you can navigate to a storage location and open previously saved documents. Once a document is open, you can edit or print it.

Opening Older Word Documents

If you open a document created in a previous version of Word, it opens in Compatibility Mode. The term appears in the Title Bar. Older Word documents do not understand the new features in Word 2007, so those features are limited or disabled.

Storing Your Exercise Files

Throughout this book you will be referred to files in a folder that corresponds to the lesson number you are studying (for example, "the Lesson 02 folder"). You can store your exercise files on various media such as a USB flash drive, the My Documents folder, or a network drive at a school or company. While some figures in exercises may display files on a USB flash drive, it is assumed that you will substitute your own location for that shown in the figure.

Hands-On 1.2   Open a Document

Before You Begin: Navigate to the student web page for this book (labpub.com/learn/word07_fastcourse1) and download the student exercise files used for this book.

1. Follow these steps to open the document:

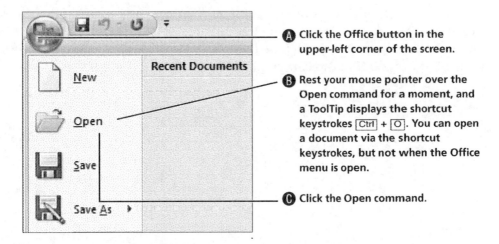

Ⓐ Click the Office button in the upper-left corner of the screen.

Ⓑ Rest your mouse pointer over the Open command for a moment, and a ToolTip displays the shortcut keystrokes Ctrl + O. You can open a document via the shortcut keystrokes, but not when the Office menu is open.

Ⓒ Click the Open command.

2. When the Open dialog box appears, follow these steps to open the Managing Diabetes document:

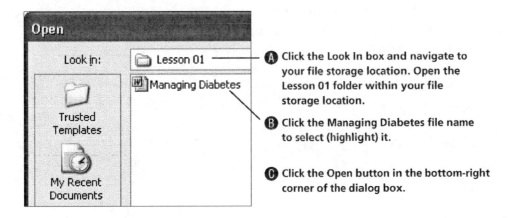

Ⓐ Click the Look In box and navigate to your file storage location. Open the Lesson 01 folder within your file storage location.

Ⓑ Click the Managing Diabetes file name to select (highlight) it.

Ⓒ Click the Open button in the bottom-right corner of the dialog box.

3. Make sure the Word window is maximized [□].

Working with the Word 2007 Interface

The band running across the top of the screen is the Ribbon. This is where you will find the tools for building, formatting, and editing your documents.

The Ribbon

The Ribbon consists of three primary areas: tabs, groups, and commands. The tabs include Home, Insert, Page Layout, and so on. A group houses related commands within a tab. Groups on the Home tab, for instance, include Clipboard, Font, Paragraph, Styles, and Editing. An example of a command in the Paragraph group is Increase Indent.

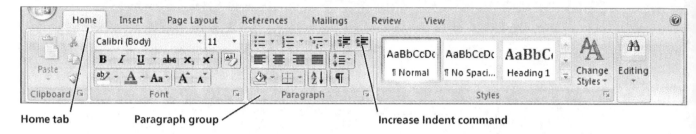

Home tab   Paragraph group   Increase Indent command

Be aware that the arrangement of the buttons on the Ribbon can vary, depending on your screen resolution and how the Word window is sized.

Contextual Tabs

Contextual tabs appear in context with the task you are performing. As shown in the following illustration, double-clicking a clip art object in a document activates Picture Tools, with the Format tab in the foreground.

Dialog Box Launcher

Some groups include a Dialog Box Launcher in the bottom-right corner of the group. This means that there are additional commands available for the group. Clicking the launcher opens the dialog box, or it may open a task pane, which, like a dialog box, houses additional related to the group.

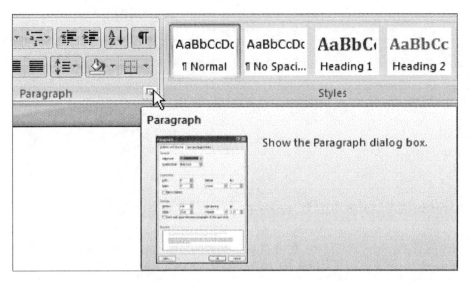

The dialog box launcher displays dialog or task panes boxes available for a given command.

Live Preview with Galleries

Live Preview shows what a formatting change looks like without actually applying the format. In the following example, selecting a block of text, and then hovering the mouse pointer over a font in the font gallery, previews how the text will look. Clicking the font name applies the font to the text.

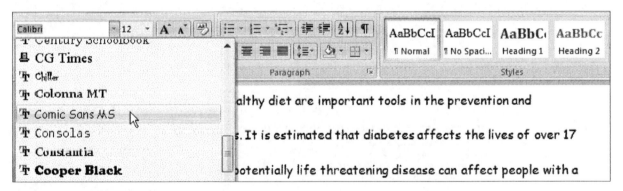

Live Preview of the Comic Sans MS Font

Hide the Ribbon

If you want more room to work, you can temporarily hide the Ribbon by double-clicking one of its tabs.

FROM THE KEYBOARD
Ctrl+F1 to hide/unhide the Ribbon

Clicking a tab, such as Home, redisplays the full Ribbon temporarily. It collapses again when you click in the document. If you want the Ribbon to remain open, right-click on the Ribbon and choose Minimize the Ribbon to turn off the feature.

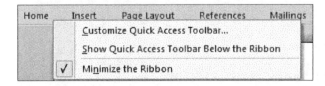

1. Click the Insert tab on the Ribbon to display the commands available in that category.

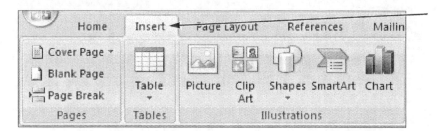

2. Take a moment to investigate some of the other tabs on the Ribbon, and then return to the Home tab.

3. Double-click the clip art object at the top of your document to display the Picture Tools on the Ribbon.

Selection handles (small circles and squares) surround an object when you click it.

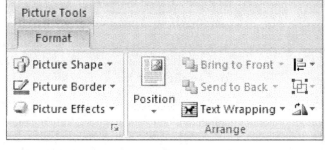

Picture Tools

4. Return to the Home tab, and hover the mouse pointer over the Dialog Box Launcher in the bottom-right corner of the Font group to display the ToolTip, as shown here.

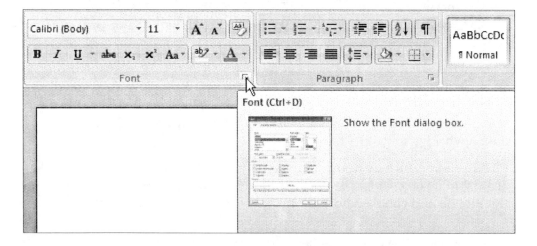

5. Click the launcher to open the Font dialog box.

6. Click the Cancel button in the bottom-right corner to close the dialog box.

7. Position the mouse pointer at the beginning of the first paragraph, press and hold the mouse button, drag to the end of the paragraph to select (highlight) it, and then release the mouse button.

8. Follow these steps to use Live Preview:

Ⓐ Click the drop-down arrow on the Font list.

Ⓑ With the mouse pointer, drag the scroll box up to the top of the scroll bar.

Ⓒ Slide the mouse pointer up to Arial Black.

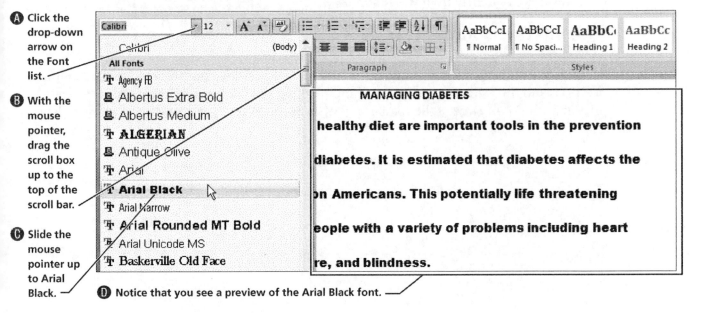

Ⓓ Notice that you see a preview of the Arial Black font.

9. Take a moment to preview a few other fonts.

10. Click anywhere in the document to close the font list, and deselect the highlighted text.

11. Double-click the Home tab to hide the Ribbon.

12. Right-click the collapsed Ribbon and choose Minimize the Ribbon from the menu to turn off the feature.

The Quick Access Toolbar

The Quick Access toolbar in the upper-left corner of the screen contains frequently used commands. It is customizable and operates independently from the Ribbon.

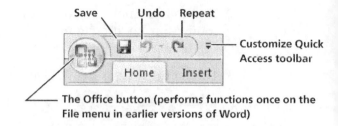

Moving the Quick Access Toolbar

You can place the Quick Access toolbar in one of two positions on the screen. The default position is to the right of the Office button. Clicking the Customize Quick Access toolbar button at the right edge of the toolbar reveals a menu where you can choose Show Below the Ribbon.

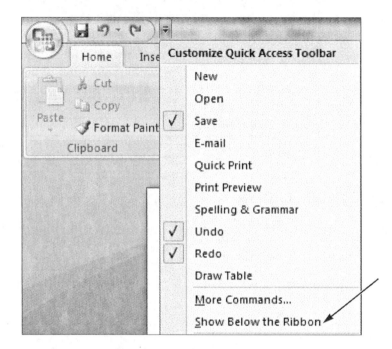

Customizing the Quick Access Toolbar

You can add buttons to and remove them from the Quick Access toolbar to suit your needs. You might want to add commands you use regularly so they are always available.

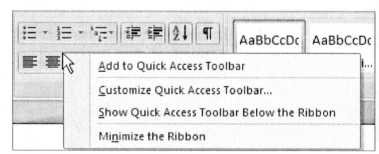

Right-click the Ribbon command you want to add (Center in this example), and choose Add to Quick Access Toolbar from the shortcut menu.

To remove a button from the Quick Access toolbar, right-click the button and choose Remove from Quick Access Toolbar from the shortcut menu.

1. Follow these steps to move the Quick Access toolbar below the Ribbon:

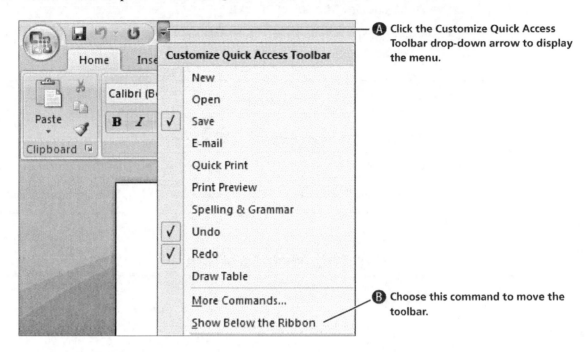

Ⓐ Click the Customize Quick Access Toolbar drop-down arrow to display the menu.

Ⓑ Choose this command to move the toolbar.

2. Click the drop-down arrow at the right edge of the Quick Access toolbar again, and this time choose Show Above the Ribbon.

3. Make sure that the Home tab is in the foreground, and then follow these steps to add the Bullets button to the toolbar:

Ⓐ Right-click the Bullets button in the Paragraph group to display the shortcut menu.

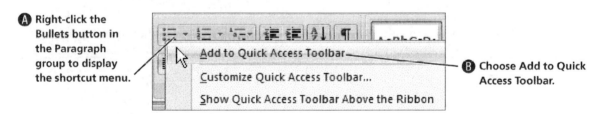

Ⓑ Choose Add to Quick Access Toolbar.

4. Right-click the Bullets ⠿ button on the Quick Access toolbar and choose the Remove from Quick Access Toolbar command.

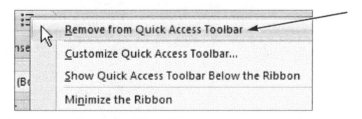

The Mini Toolbar

There's another toolbar in Word, and it contains frequently used formatting commands. When you select (highlight) text, the Mini toolbar fades in. After a pause, it fades away. Make it reappear by right-clicking the selected text.

In the following example, clicking the Bold **B** button on the Mini toolbar applies the Bold feature to the selected text.

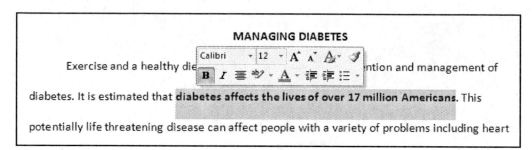

 Hands-On 1.5   **Use the Mini Toolbar**

1. Follow these steps to italicize a word:

A Double-click the word *Exercise* at the start of the paragraph to select (highlight) it.

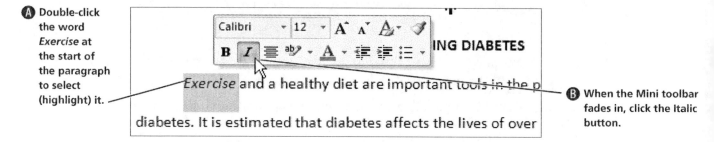

B When the Mini toolbar fades in, click the Italic button.

2. Click anywhere in the document to deselect the text and view the formatted word.

Navigating in a Word Document

If you are working in a multipage document, it is helpful to know about various techniques for moving through a document. You can navigate using the scroll bar located at the right side of the screen, or you can use keystrokes.

Navigating with the Scroll Bar

The scroll bar lets you browse through documents; however, it does not move the cursor. After scrolling, you must click in the document to reposition the cursor. The following illustration shows the components of the scroll bar.

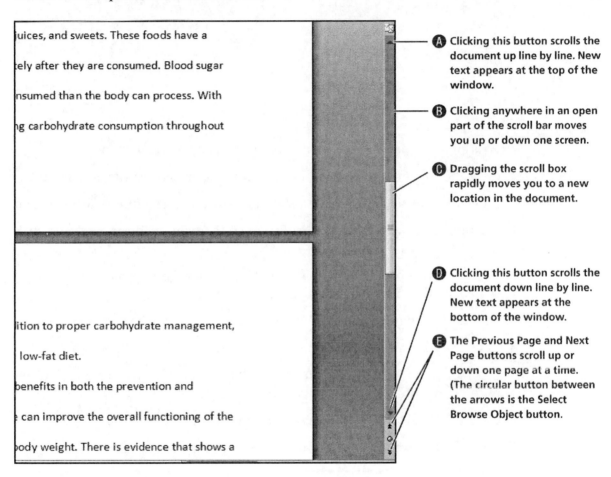

juices, and sweets. These foods have a

tely after they are consumed. Blood sugar

nsumed than the body can process. With

ng carbohydrate consumption throughout

A Clicking this button scrolls the document up line by line. New text appears at the top of the window.

B Clicking anywhere in an open part of the scroll bar moves you up or down one screen.

C Dragging the scroll box rapidly moves you to a new location in the document.

ition to proper carbohydrate management,

low-fat diet.

benefits in both the prevention and

can improve the overall functioning of the

body weight. There is evidence that shows a

D Clicking this button scrolls the document down line by line. New text appears at the bottom of the window.

E The Previous Page and Next Page buttons scroll up or down one page at a time. (The circular button between the arrows is the Select Browse Object button.

1. Follow these steps to scroll in the document:

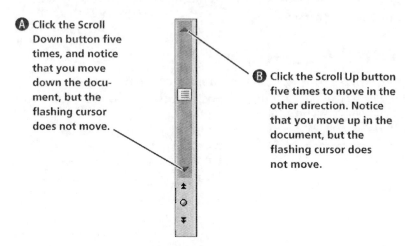

A Click the Scroll Down button five times, and notice that you move down the document, but the flashing cursor does not move.

B Click the Scroll Up button five times to move in the other direction. Notice that you move up in the document, but the flashing cursor does not move.

2. Position the I-beam I mouse pointer in the body of the document.

3. Click the I-beam I anywhere in the document to position the blinking cursor.

4. Move the mouse pointer into the left margin area. The white ⇗ arrow shape is now visible.

5. Position the I-beam I in the first line of the body of the document, and click the left mouse button.

6. Click the open part of the scroll bar below the scroll box to move down one screen, as shown in the illustration to the right.

7. Drag the scroll box to the bottom of the scroll bar with the mouse pointer.

8. Click the I-beam I at the end of the text to position it on the last page.

9. Drag the scroll box to the top of the scroll bar, and click the I-beam I in front of the first word of the first paragraph.

10. Click the Next Page ⬇ button to move to the top of page 2.

11. Click the Previous Page ⬆ button to move to the top of page 1.

Navigating with the Keyboard

Whether you use the mouse or the keyboard to navigate through a document is a matter of personal preference. Navigating with the keyboard always moves the cursor, so it will be with you when you arrive at your destination.

 Hands-On 1.7   Use the Keyboard to Navigate

1. Click the I-beam I in the middle of the first line of the first paragraph.

2. Tap the right arrow → and left arrow ← keys a few times to move to the right and left, one character at a time.

3. Tap the down arrow ↓ and up arrow ↑ keys a few times to move down, one row at a time.

4. Hold down the Ctrl key and keep it down, then tap the Home key to move to the beginning of the document. Release the Ctrl key.

5. Use the arrow keys to position the cursor in the middle of the first line of the first paragraph.

6. Hold down the Ctrl key and keep it down, then tap the left arrow ← key a few times to move to the left, one word at a time. Release the Ctrl key.

7. Hold down the Ctrl key and keep it down, then tap the right arrow → key several times to move to the right, one word at a time. Release the Ctrl key.

8. Tap the Home key to move to the beginning of the line.

9. Tap the End key to move to the end of the line.

10. Spend a few moments navigating with the keyboard.

Closing Documents

You close a file by clicking the Office button and choosing the Close command from the menu. If you haven't saved your document, Word will prompt you to save it.

 Hands-On 1.8   Close the Document

1. Click the Office button, and then choose Close from the menu.

2. When Word asks you if you want to save the changes, click No.

3. If a blank document is open on the screen, use the same technique to close it.

Starting a New Blank Document

FROM THE KEYBOARD

Ctrl + N to start a new document

When all documents are closed, you can click the Office button, and then choose the New command from the menu to open a new blank document.

 Hands-On 1.9   **Start a New Document**

1. Click the Office button, and then choose New from the menu.

2. When the New Document dialog box appears, click the Create button in the bottom-right corner to display the new document.

3. Click the Office button, and then choose Close from the menu.

4. Hold down the Ctrl key and tap the N on your keyboard to open a new document.

5. Leave this document open.

Exiting from Word

Clicking the Office button and then clicking the ✕ Exit Word button closes the Word application. It's important to exit Word in an orderly fashion. Turning off your computer before exiting Word could cause you to lose data.

 Hands-On 1.10   **Exit from Word**

1. Click the Office button.

2. Click the ✕ Exit Word button in the bottom-right corner of the window.

3. If Word prompts you to save changes, click No.

Concepts Review

True/False Questions

1. The cursor automatically repositions when you scroll through a document using the scroll bars.   **TRUE   FALSE**

2. The Mini toolbar appears in the upper-left corner of the Word screen.   **TRUE   FALSE**

3. A Dialog Box Launcher leads to additional commands for a group on the Ribbon.   **TRUE   FALSE**

4. The band running across the top of the Word screen is known as the Ribbon.   **TRUE   FALSE**

5. Tapping the Home key always moves the cursor to the top of the document.   **TRUE   FALSE**

6. Contextual tabs appear in context with the task you are performing.   **TRUE   FALSE**

7. The `Page Down` key on your keyboard moves you down though a document one page at a time.   **TRUE   FALSE**

8. If you open a document created in a previous version of Word, the term Compatibility Mode appears in the title bar.   **TRUE   FALSE**

9. The Quick Access toolbar works in conjunction with the Ribbon; therefore, it is not customizable.   **TRUE   FALSE**

10. Tabs on the Ribbon, such as the Home tab, are divided into command groups.   **TRUE   FALSE**

Multiple Choice Questions

1. Which of the following terms does not relate to the Ribbon?
   a. Contextual tabs
   b. Undo
   c. Dialog Box Launcher
   d. Galleries

2. Which of the following commands is correct regarding keyboard navigation?
   a. `Alt`+`→` moves the cursor one word to the right.
   b. `Ctrl`+`End` moves the cursor to the end of the document.
   c. `Home` moves the cursor to the beginning of the previous paragraph.
   d. `Alt`+`End` moves the cursor to the end of the line.

3. Word provides the capability to view what formatting changes would look like without actually applying the format. That feature is known as _____.
   a. Formatting Ribbon
   b. Contextual tabs
   c. Print Preview
   d. Live Preview

4. Which of the following statements is correct regarding the Mini Toolbar?
   a. It's located on the Home tab of the Ribbon.
   b. It is customizable.
   c. It appears when you select text.
   d. You hold down the `Ctrl` key and tap `M` to display it.

Creating and Editing Business Letters

In this lesson, you will create business letters while learning proper business document formatting. You will also learn fundamental techniques of entering and editing text, copying and moving text, and saving and printing documents. In addition, you will learn to use Word's AutoCorrect tool to insert frequently used text.

LESSON OBJECTIVES

After studying this lesson, you will be able to:

- Type a professional business letter
- Save a document
- Select and edit text
- Use the AutoCorrect feature
- Copy and move text
- Print a document

LESSON TIMING

- Concepts/Hands-On: 1 hr 15 min
- Concepts Review: 15 min
- Total: 1 hr 30 min

CASE STUDY: TAKING CARE WITH BUSINESS LETTERS

Terrel Richardson just landed his first job as a medical assistant in the Cardiology Department at St. Mary's Hospital. He is working for Dr. Wright, a cardiologist in the Electrophysiology Lab. A primary care physician is referring one of his patients to the lab for an ablation procedure. Dr. Wright asked Terrel to prepare a standard letter for patients orienting them to the department and providing information about the procedure.

Terrel starts by referring to his business writing class textbook to ensure that he formats the letter correctly for a good first impression and a professional appearance.

Inserting Text

You always insert text into a Word document at the flashing cursor. Therefore, you must position the cursor at the desired location before typing.

AutoComplete

Word's AutoComplete feature does some of your typing for you. It recognizes certain words and phrases, such as names of months and names of days, and offers to complete them for you, as shown here.

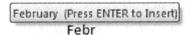

February (Press ENTER to Insert)
Febr

As you begin typing the month Febr, AutoComplete offers to finish typing it out.

You accept AutoComplete suggestions by tapping [Enter]. If you choose to ignore the suggestion, just keep typing, and the suggestion will disappear.

Using the Enter Key

You use [Enter] to begin a new paragraph or to insert blank lines in a document. Word considers anything that ends by tapping [Enter] to be a paragraph. Thus, short lines such as a date line, an inside address, or even blank lines themselves are considered paragraphs.

Tapping [Enter] inserts a paragraph ¶ symbol in a document. These symbols are visible when you display formatting marks.

Showing Formatting Marks

The Show/Hide ¶ button in the Paragraph group of the Home tab shows or hides formatting marks. Although they appear on the screen, you will not see them in the printed document. Marks include dots representing spaces between words, paragraph symbols that appear when you tap [Enter], and arrows that represent tabs.

Viewing these characters can be important when editing a document. You may need to see the nonprinting characters to determine whether the space between two words was created with the [Spacebar] or [Tab]. The following illustrations show the location of the Show/Hide button and the characters that appear when you tap the [Spacebar], the [Enter] key, or the [Tab].

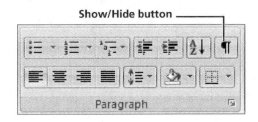

Show/Hide button

Paragraph

These symbols are paragraph marks. They appear whenever you tap [Enter].

The dots between words are inserted when you tap the [Spacebar].

Tabs are represented by small arrows.

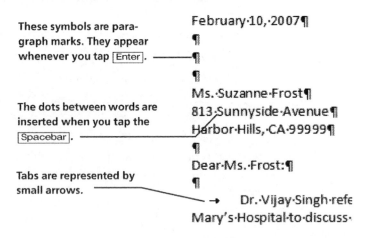

February·10,·2007¶
¶
¶
¶
Ms.·Suzanne·Frost¶
813·Sunnyside·Avenue¶
Harbor·Hills,·CA·99999¶
¶
Dear·Ms.·Frost:¶
¶
→   Dr.·Vijay·Singh·refe
Mary's·Hospital·to·discuss·

Spacing in Letters

Word 2007 introduces a new default line spacing. Rather than a default of single spacing, which has been the standard for word processors from the beginning, Word 2007 introduces 1.15 line spacing. This additional space can make your documents easier to read. The new spacing also includes an extra 10 points of space at the end of paragraphs. (That's a little over an eighth of an inch.) Rather than tapping [Enter] twice at the end of a paragraph, just tap [Enter] once, and Word adds the extra spacing.

Apply Traditional Spacing Using the Line Spacing Button

When writing letters, a traditional, more compact look (without the additional spacing) is still considered appropriate. Therefore, when you begin a letter, you may wish to switch to single (1.0) spacing and remove the extra space after paragraphs by choosing the options shown in the following figure.

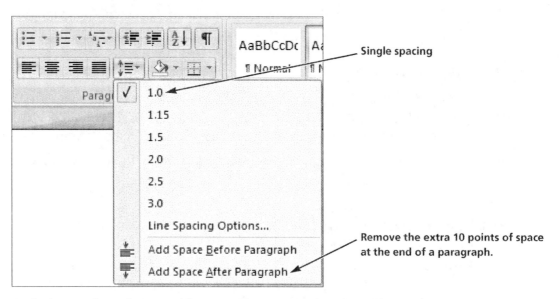

Apply these settings when you wish to type a more compact, traditional letter.

Apply Traditional Spacing Using the No Spacing Style

An alternative to using the Line Spacing button to achieve traditional spacing is to apply the No Spacing style located in the Styles group of the Home tab on the Ribbon, as shown here.

When you begin a new document, click the No Spacing icon on the Ribbon to achieve traditional spacing. The concept of Word's Styles feature is covered in detail in *FastCourse Word 2007: Level 2*.

Word Wrap

If you continue typing after the cursor reaches the end of a line, Word automatically wraps the cursor to the beginning of the next line. If you let Word Wrap format your paragraph initially, the paragraph will also reformat correctly as you insert or delete text.

 Hands-On 2.1   Type a Letter

1. Start Word. Make sure the Word window is maximized ⬜.

2. Choose Home→Paragraph→Show/Hide ¶ from the Ribbon.

3. Position the I-beam Ⅰ left of the paragraph symbol, press and hold the mouse button, drag to the right to select (highlight)the paragraph symbol, and then release the mouse button.

4. Follow these steps to reformat the paragraph symbol:

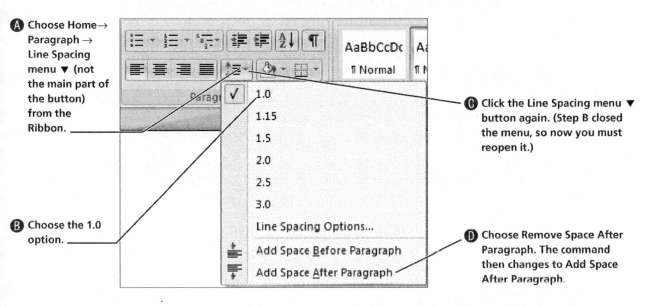

A Choose Home→ Paragraph → Line Spacing menu ▼ (not the main part of the button) from the Ribbon.

B Choose the 1.0 option.

C Click the Line Spacing menu ▼ button again. (Step B closed the menu, so now you must reopen it.)

D Choose Remove Space After Paragraph. The command then changes to Add Space After Paragraph.

5. Click the View Ruler 🔲 button at the top of the vertical scroll bar to display the ruler.

6. Tap ⌊Enter⌋ six times to place the cursor 2 inches from the top of the page (at approximately the 1 inch mark on the vertical ruler).

7. Start typing **Febr,** but stop when AutoComplete displays a pop-up tip.

8. Tap ⌊Enter⌋ to automatically insert February into the letter.

9. Finish typing the date as **February 10, 2007**.

10. Continue typing the letter as shown at right, tapping ⌊Enter⌋ wherever you see a paragraph symbol. If you catch a typo, you can tap the ⌊Backspace⌋ key enough times to remove the error, and then continue typing.

11. Type the first body paragraph in the following illustration. Let Word Wrap do its thing, and then tap ⌊Enter⌋ twice at the end of the paragraph. Continue typing the letter, tapping ⌊Enter⌋ where you see a paragraph symbol.

¶
¶
¶
¶
¶
¶
February·10,·2007¶
¶
¶
¶
Ms.·Suzanne·Frost¶
813·Sunnyside·Avenue¶
Harbor·Hills,·CA·99999¶
¶
Dear·Ms.·Frost:¶
¶
¶

Dear·Ms.·Frost:¶
¶
Dr.·Vijay·Singh·has·referred·you·to·us·for·a·consultation·in·the·Electrophysiology·Department·at·St.·Mary's·Hospital·to·discuss·an·ablation·procedure.·Catheter·ablation·is·a·non-surgical·technique·that·destroys·parts·of·the·abnormal·electrical·pathway·that·is·causing·your·arrhythmia.·¶
¶
Enclosed·please·find·informational·materials·for·your·review·regarding·this·procedure.·After·reading·the·booklets,·please·contact·our·office·ASAP·so·that·we·can·discuss·your·options.¶
¶
Yours·truly,¶
¶
¶
¶
Terrel·Richardson¶
Medical·Assistant¶
Electrophysiology·Department¶
¶
¶

12. Choose Home→Paragraph→Show/Hide ¶ to turn off formatting marks.

Saving Your Work

It's important to save your documents frequently! Power outages and accidents can result in lost data. Documents are saved to storage locations such as hard drives and USB flash drives.

The Save Command

There are three primary commands used to save Word documents:

FROM THE KEYBOARD

Ctrl+S to save

- The Save [icon] button on the Quick Access toolbar

- The Office [icon] →Save command

- The Office [icon] →Save As command

When you save a document for the first time, the Save As dialog box appears. The following illustration describes significant features of the Save As dialog box.

You can choose a storage location by navigating in the Save In list or by clicking a button on the My Places bar, which houses frequently used storage locations.

Go to a previous storage location.

Move up one level in the storage hierarchy.

Delete the selected file or folder.

Change the view.

Create a new folder.

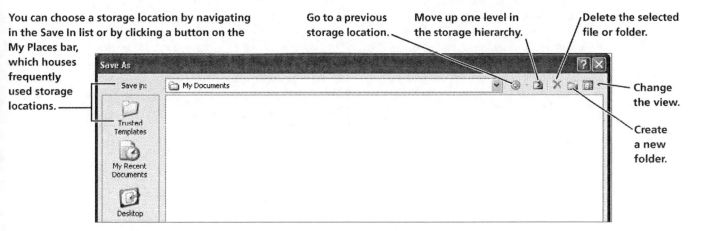

Save Compared to Save As

While the Save and Save As commands are quite similar, each has a specific use. If the document was never saved, Word displays the Save As dialog box, where you specify the name and storage location of the document. If the document was previously saved, choosing the save command again replaces the prior version with the edited one, without displaying the Save As dialog box.

Word's DOCX File Format

A file format is a technique for saving computer data. Previous versions of Word saved documents in the *doc* format. Word 2007 introduces a new file format: *docx*. This is important because users of earlier versions of Word may not be able to read Word files in the new docx file format without installing special software.

Hands-On 2.2   Save the Letter

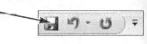

1. Click the Save ⊟ button on the Quick Access toolbar. Word displays the Save As dialog box, since this is the first time you are saving this document. Once the file is named, this button will simply save the current version of the file over the old version.

2. Follow these steps to save the letter:

Ⓐ Click the Save In box, and open the Lesson 02 folder on your file storage location.

Ⓑ Word always proposes the first line of text as the filename. Type the name **Frost Letter** and it will replace the proposed name. (If you switched file storage locations, you may need to click in the File Name box, delete the proposed name with the Delete or Backspace key, and then type the new name.)

Ⓒ Click the Save button.

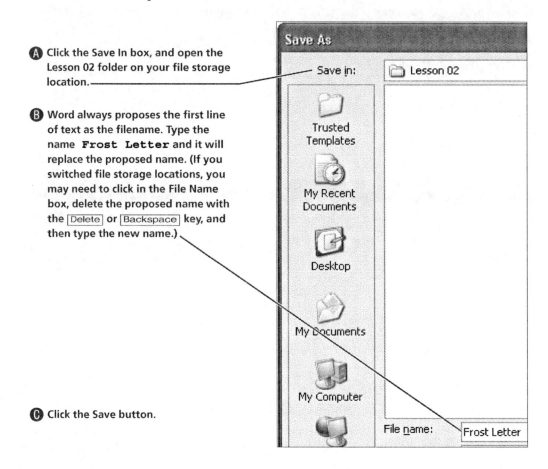

3. Leave the file open for the next exercise.

Selecting Text

You must select (highlight) text if you wish to perform some action on it. Suppose you want to delete an entire line. You would select the line first, and then tap Delete.

Selection Techniques

Word provides many selection techniques; some use the mouse, and some use the keyboard. Beginners may find the mouse difficult to control; keyboard techniques tend to provide greater control. Use the keyboard techniques if you have difficulty controlling the mouse. Deselect text by clicking in the white background of the document or by tapping an arrow key.

1. Follow these steps to select text using the left margin:

Ⓐ Point outside the margin of the first line until the mouse pointer tilts slightly to the right, as shown here.

Ⓑ Click once to select the entire line.

Ms. Suzanne Frost
813 Sunnyside Avenue
Harbor Hills, CA 99999

Ⓒ Make sure the pointer tilts to the right, and then click once to select this line. (Notice that the previously selected line is no longer selected.)

Dear Ms. Frost:

Dr. Vijay Singh has referred you to us for consultation in the Electrophysiology Department at St. Mary's Hospital to discuss an ablation procedure. Catheter ablation is a non-surgical technique that destroys parts of the abnormal electrical pathway that is causing your arrhythmia.

Ⓓ Select this paragraph by double-clicking in front of it, using the white selection arrow.

2. Making sure the mouse pointer tilts to the right 🖱, drag down the left margin. Be sure to press and hold the left mouse button as you drag. Then, click in the body of the document to deselect the text.

3. Move the mouse pointer back to the margin so it is tilting to the right 🖱 and outside the margin, then triple-click anywhere in the left margin.

4. Click once anywhere in the body of the document to deselect it.

5. Point on any word with the I-beam Ⅰ, and then double-click to select it.

6. Double-click a different word, and notice that the previous word is deselected.

7. Double-click to select one word.

8. With one word selected, press and hold the ⒞Ctrl key while you double-click to select another word, and then release the ⒞Ctrl key.

9. Follow these steps to drag and select a block of text:

Ⓐ Position the I-beam here, just in front of *Dr. Vijay Singh*…. Make sure the I-beam is visible, not the right-tilting arrow.

Ⓑ Press and hold down the mouse button, and then drag to the right until the phrase *Dr. Vijay Singh has referred you to us for a consultation* is selected.

Ⅰ Dr. Vijay Singh has referred you to us for a consultation in the Hospital to discuss an ablation procedure. Catheter ablation is parts of the abnormal electrical pathway that is causing your a

Ⓒ Release the mouse button; the text remains selected.

Editing Text

Word offers many tools for editing documents, allowing you to insert and delete text and undo and redo work.

Insert and Delete Text

When you insert text in Word, existing text moves to the right as you type. You must position the cursor before you begin typing.

Use [Backspace] and [Delete] to remove text. The [Backspace] key deletes *back* to the left of the cursor. The [Delete] key removes characters to the *right* of the cursor. You can also remove an entire block of text by selecting it, and then tapping [Delete] or [Backspace].

Use Undo and Redo

FROM THE KEYBOARD

[Ctrl]+[Z] to undo the last action

Word's Undo button lets you reverse your last editing or formatting change(s). You can reverse simple actions such as accidental text deletions, or you can reverse more complex actions, such as margin changes.

The Redo ⟳ button reverses Undo. Use Redo when you undo an action and then change your mind.

The Undo menu ▾ button (see figure at right) displays a list of recent changes. You can undo multiple actions by dragging the mouse pointer over the desired items in the list. However, you must undo changes in the order in which they appear on the list.

🖱 Hands-On 2.4   Insert and Delete Text and Use Undo and Redo

1. In the first line of the first paragraph, double-click the word *has*, as shown to the right, and then tap [Delete] to remove the word.

2. Click with the I-beam (not the right-tilted arrow) at the beginning of the third line of the first paragraph, and type **(ablates)**, and then tap the [Spacebar].

   > Dear Ms. Frost:
   >
   > Dr. Vijay Singh has referred
   > Mary's Hospital to discuss a

3. Position the cursor at the end of the first paragraph between *arrhythmia* and the period at the end of the sentence.

4. Tap the [Spacebar], and type **(abnormal heart rhythm)**.

5. Drag to select the first three words of the second paragraph as shown, and then type **I have enclosed** to replace the selected text.

   > Enclosed please find informational
   > Booklets, please contact our office

6. Click with the I-beam after the next word, *informational*, and tap [Backspace] twice to change the word to *information*.

---

7. Double-click the next word, *materials*, and tap [Delete] to remove it.

8. In the next line, double-click *ASAP*, and type **at your earliest convenience**, in its place.

9. In the same line, double-click *that* and tap [Delete].

10. Move the mouse pointer into the margin to the left of *Yours truly*. Remember, the mouse pointer is a white arrow when it's in the left margin.

11. Click once to select the line, and then type **Sincerely,** in its place.

12. You've decided that you prefer *Yours truly*, so click the Undo [↶] button on the Quick Access toolbar to return to *Yours truly*.

13. Well, maybe *Sincerely* is better after all. Click the Redo [↷] button on the Quick Access toolbar to return to *Sincerely*.

14. Click the Save [💾] button on the Quick Access toolbar to save your changes.

15. Leave the document open for the next exercise.

Working with AutoCorrect

AutoCorrect is predefined text used for automatically correcting common spelling and capitalization errors. You may have noticed AutoCorrect changing the spelling of certain words while working through this course.

Word's AutoCorrect feature corrects more than spelling errors. For example, you could set up AutoCorrect to insert the phrase *as soon as possible* whenever you type *asap* and tap the [Spacebar]. AutoCorrect will also capitalize a word it thinks is the beginning of a sentence.

Hands-On 2.5   Use AutoCorrect

1. Tap [Ctrl]+[End] to move the cursor to the end of the document.

2. If necessary, tap [Enter] a few times to provide some space to practice.

3. Type the word **teh** and tap the [Spacebar].

4. Type the word **adn** and tap the [Spacebar].

5. Now select and [Delete] the words you were just practicing with.

AutoCorrect Options Smart Tag

Word uses smart tags, small buttons that pop up automatically, to provide menus of options that are in context with what you are doing at the time. One of those smart tags is the AutoCorrect Options smart tag.

If Word automatically corrects something that you don't want corrected, a smart tag option allows you to undo the change. For example, when Word automatically capitalizes the first C in the cc: line, you can quickly undo the capitalization.

 Hands-On 2.6   Use the AutoCorrect Smart Tag

1. Choose Home→Paragraph→Show/Hide ¶ to display formatting marks.

   Terrell·Richardson¶
   Medical·Assistant¶
   Electrophysiology·Department¶
   ¶
   ¶

2. If necessary, position the cursor and use Enter to create the blank line(s).

3. Position the cursor next to the second paragraph symbol, and type **tr** as the reference initials, and then tap Enter.

4. Position the mouse pointer over the T, and you should see a small blue rectangle just below the T. Then drag down a little, and the AutoCorrect Options screen tip appears.

5. Click the AutoCorrect Options smart tag to display the menu shown below. (This is a delicate mouse move, so you may need to try it a couple of times.)

   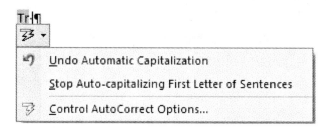

6. Choose Undo Automatic Capitalization from the menu.

7. Make sure the cursor is on the blank line below the initials. Then type the enclosures notification, **Enclosures (2)**, and tap Enter.

8. Save the document and leave it open for the next exercise.

Setting AutoCorrect Options

To open the AutoCorrect dialog box, choose Office 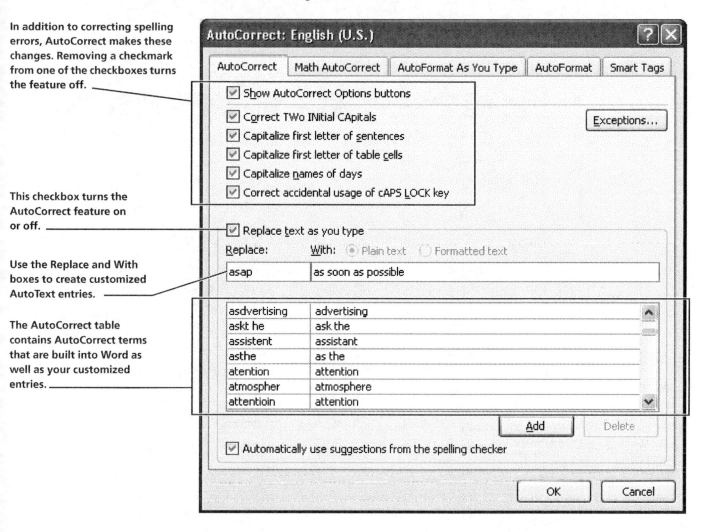, and then click the Word Options button to display the Word Options window. Choose Proofing from the menu on the left, and then click the AutoCorrect Options button.

In addition to correcting spelling errors, AutoCorrect makes these changes. Removing a checkmark from one of the checkboxes turns the feature off.

This checkbox turns the AutoCorrect feature on or off.

Use the Replace and With boxes to create customized AutoText entries.

The AutoCorrect table contains AutoCorrect terms that are built into Word as well as your customized entries.

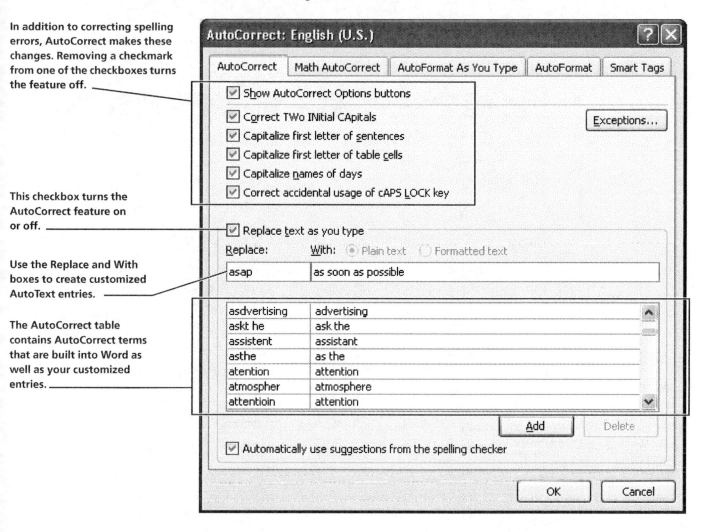

Customizing AutoCorrect

Word's AutoCorrect feature also lets you automatically insert customized text and special characters, and it is useful for replacing abbreviations with full phrases. For example you could set up AutoCorrect to insert the phrase *as soon as possible* whenever you type *asap*.

Hands-On 2.7   Create a Custom AutoCorrect Entry

1. Click the Office button, and then click the Word Options button in the bottom-right corner of the window.

2. When the Word Options window opens, follow these steps to display the AutoCorrect dialog box:

A Choose the Proofing category.

B Click the AutoCorrect Options button.

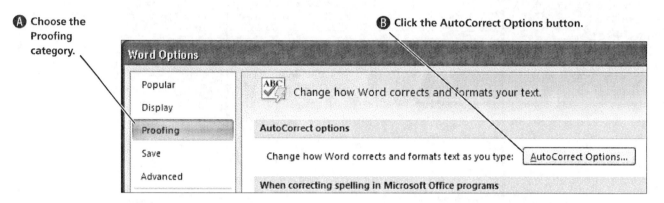

3. When the AutoCorrect dialog box appears, follow these steps to add a custom AutoCorrect entry:

A Type **dw** in the Replace box.

B Type **Dr. Marjorie Wright** in the With box.

C Click the Add button.

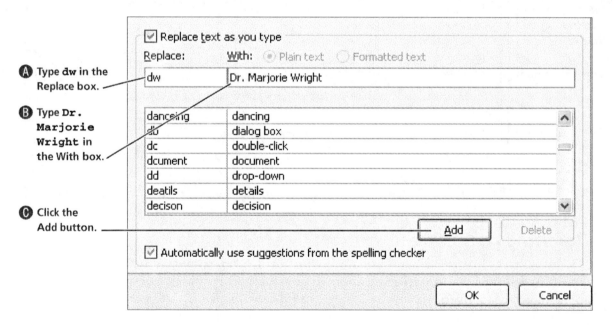

4. Click OK twice.

5. Type **cc:** and tap the Spacebar.

6. Use the AutoCorrect Options smart tag to undo the automatic capitalization.

7. Type **dw** and tap Enter to automatically type the doctor's name.

8. Click the Office button, and then click the Word Options button in the bottom-right corner of the window.

9. Choose Proofing from the menu, and then click the AutoCorrect Options button in the right-hand pane.

10. Type **dw** in the Replace box, which scrolls the list to Dr. Marjorie Wright.

11. Click the Delete button in the bottom-right corner of the dialog box.

12. Click OK twice.

13. Save the letter and leave it open for the next exercise.

Copying and Moving Text

Cut, Copy, and Paste allow you to copy and move text within a document or between documents. The Cut, Copy, and Paste commands are conveniently located on the Ribbon in the Clipboard command group at the left side of the Home tab.

FROM THE KEYBOARD
Ctrl+C to copy
Ctrl+X to cut
Ctrl+V to paste

Hands-On 2.8   Use Cut, Copy, and Paste

1. If necessary, choose Home→Paragraph→Show/Hide ¶ from the Ribbon to display the formatting marks.

2. Position the mouse pointer in the margin to the left of the date, and then click once to select the line.

3. Choose Home→Clipboard→Copy from the Ribbon.

4. Tap Ctrl+End to place the cursor at the bottom of the document.

5. If necessary, tap Enter a couple of times to provide some blank space at the bottom of the document.

6. Choose Home→Clipboard→Paste from the Ribbon to place a copy of the date at the bottom of the document.

7. Click the smart tag to view its menu, and then click in the document background to close the menu.

8. Tap the Esc key to dismiss the button.

9. Click the Undo button to undo the paste.

10. Position the mouse pointer in the margin to the left of the first line of the inside address, and then press and hold down the mouse button and drag to select all three lines.

11. Choose Home→Clipboard→Cut from the Ribbon.

12. Tap Ctrl+End to move the cursor to the bottom of the document.

13. Tap Enter if you need space.

14. Tap Ctrl+V to paste the text.

15. Tap Esc to dismiss the Paste Options smart tag.

16. Scroll up and notice that the address no longer appears at the top of the document.

17. Click the Undo ↺ twice to undo the move.

18. Click the Save 🖫 button to save your changes.

Editing with Drag and Drop

Drag and drop produces the same result as cut, copy, and paste. It is efficient for moving or copying text a short distance within the same page. You select the text you wish to move and then drag it to the desired destination. If you press and hold [Ctrl] while dragging, the text is copied to the destination.

 Hands-On 2.9   Use Drag and Drop

1. Make sure there are a couple of blank lines at the bottom of your document.

2. If necessary, scroll so that you can see both the bottom of the document and the *Terrel Richardson* line in the signature block.

3. Select the *Terrel Richardson* line, and then release the mouse button.

¶
Terrel·Richardson¶
Medical·Assistant¶
Electrophysiology·Department¶
¶

4. Place the mouse pointer in the highlighted text.

5. Press and hold the mouse button, and follow these steps to move the text:

A Drag down to the bottom of the document, and when you do so, the mouse pointer has a small rectangle at the bottom indicating you are in drag-and-drop mode.

B You will also see a dotted cursor that travels with the mouse pointer. Position it at the bottom of the document.

¶
Terrel·Richardson¶
Medical·Assistant¶
Electrophysiology·Department¶
¶
tr¶
Enclosures·(2)¶
cc:·Dr.·Marjorie·Wright¶
¶
¶

C Release the mouse button to complete the move.

6. Click the Undo ↺ button to undo the move.

7. Make sure the *Terrel Richardson* line is still selected.

8. Place the mouse pointer inside the selected text, press and hold the [Ctrl] key and drag the text to the bottom of the document, release the mouse button, and then release the [Ctrl] key.

9. Click Undo ↺ to undo the copy.

10. Leave the document open for the next exercise.

The Clipboard

The Clipboard lets you collect multiple items and paste them into a document. It must be visible on the screen to assemble multiple items; otherwise, only one item at a time is saved for pasting. The Clipboard can hold up to 24 items. When you cut or copy any items exceeding 24, the Clipboard automatically deletes the oldest items.

You click the Dialog Box Launcher ▣ to display the Clipboard task pane.

The following illustration points out the features of the Clipboard.

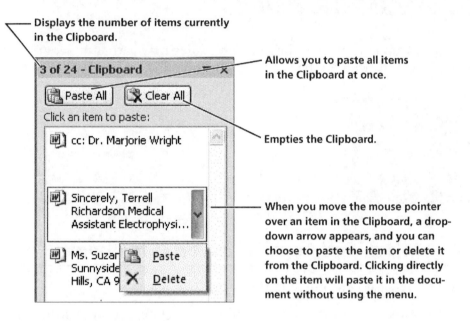

Displays the number of items currently in the Clipboard.

Allows you to paste all items in the Clipboard at once.

Empties the Clipboard.

When you move the mouse pointer over an item in the Clipboard, a drop-down arrow appears, and you can choose to paste the item or delete it from the Clipboard. Clicking directly on the item will paste it in the document without using the menu.

The Clipboard Options button at the bottom of the task pane offers useful options. Click an item in the menu to turn it on or off.

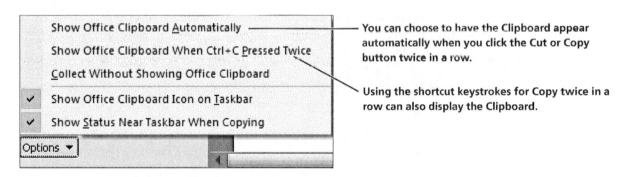

You can choose to have the Clipboard appear automatically when you click the Cut or Copy button twice in a row.

Using the shortcut keystrokes for Copy twice in a row can also display the Clipboard.

Switching Between Documents

There are several techniques for switching between documents. In the next exercise, you will use the taskbar at the bottom of the screen for switching documents. When you have multiple documents open, they will appear as icons on the taskbar. Clicking an icon displays that document in the foreground. In the following illustration, Frost Letter is the active document. The active document icon is darker than the others.

If you have several documents open at the same time, they may gather under one icon. You access them by clicking the icon on the taskbar, then choosing a document from the list.

 Hands-On 2.10   Switch and Copy Between Documents

1. Open the Medical Release document in the Lesson 02 folder.

2. Go to the taskbar and click the Frost Letter icon to switch back to that document.

3. Click the Dialog Box Launcher in the Home→Clipboard command group, to open the Clipboard task pane.

4. If there are any items in the Clipboard, click the Clear All button at the top of the task pane.

5. Select the three-line inside address, and tap [Ctrl]+[C] to copy the text to the Clipboard.

6. Select Suzanne Frost, and choose Home→Clipboard→Copy 🗐 to copy the text to the Clipboard.

7. At the beginning of the first paragraph, click and drag to select *Dr. Vijay Singh,* and then use either the shortcut keystrokes or the Copy command on the Ribbon to copy the text.

8. Select and copy the word *arrhythmia* toward the end of the first paragraph.

9. Select *Dr. Marjorie Wright* (but not the paragraph symbol that follows it) and copy the text to the Clipboard.

10. Go to the taskbar and switch to Medical Release.

11. Click the Dialog Box Launcher 🗔 on the Clipboard group of the Home tab to open the Clipboard task pane.

12. Select the first three lines in Medical Release, as shown here.

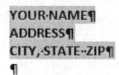

YOUR·NAME¶
ADDRESS¶
CITY,·STATE··ZIP¶
¶

13. Click the inside address in the Clipboard to paste it over the selected text.

14. Select DOCTOR NAME in the salutation, and paste *Dr. Vijay Singh* in its place.

15. The appropriate form for the salutation is title and last name, so select *Vijay* and tap Delete.

16. In the body paragraph, select DOCTOR NAME and paste *Dr. Marjorie Wright* in its place.

17. In the second line of that paragraph, select MEDICAL CONDITION and paste *arrhythmia* in its place.

18. Select YOUR NAME at the bottom of the document and paste *Suzanne Frost* in its place.

19. Click the Save 🖫 button on the Quick Access toolbar.

20. Click the Close ✕ button at the top of the Clipboard.

21. Choose Office ⊚ →Close to close Medical Release.

22. When your original letter appears, close the Clipboard.

23. Leave this document open for the next exercise.

Working with Print Preview

The Print Preview window shows how a document will look when it prints. It is especially useful when printing long documents and those containing intricate graphics and formatting. It is always wise to preview a long or complex document before sending it to the printer.

Displaying Print Preview

You display the Print Preview window by choosing Office→Print menu ▶ button, then clicking the Print Preview command.

Preview Window Features

When you display the Print Preview window, you see a Print Preview Ribbon that replaces the regular Ribbon. The following illustration describes the commands on the Ribbon.

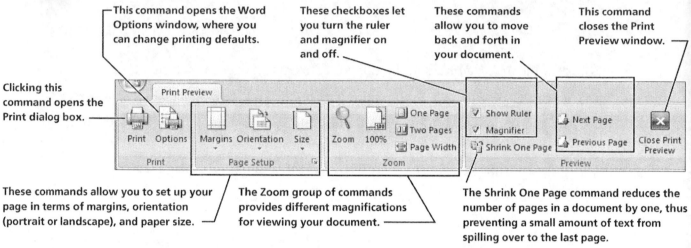

This command opens the Word Options window, where you can change printing defaults.

These checkboxes let you turn the ruler and magnifier on and off.

These commands allow you to move back and forth in your document.

This command closes the Print Preview window.

Clicking this command opens the Print dialog box.

These commands allow you to set up your page in terms of margins, orientation (portrait or landscape), and paper size.

The Zoom group of commands provides different magnifications for viewing your document.

The Shrink One Page command reduces the number of pages in a document by one, thus preventing a small amount of text from spilling over to the last page.

 Hands-On 2.11   Use Print Preview

1. Follow these steps to access the Print Preview window:

Ⓐ Click the Office button.

Ⓑ Click the Print ▸ menu command.

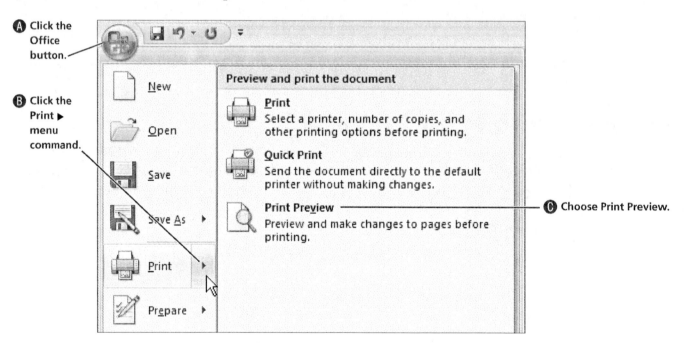

Ⓒ Choose Print Preview.

2. Position the mouse pointer over the letter, and notice that it looks like a magnifying glass.

3. Click the mouse button to magnify your letter, and then click again to zoom out.

4. Click the Zoom 🔍 button to view the Zoom dialog box.

5. Choose 200%, and then click OK.

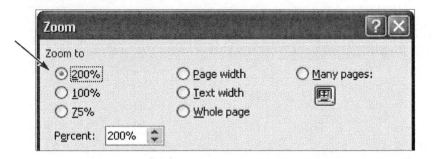

6. Click the mouse button to zoom back out.

7. Click the Page Width ▣ button on the Ribbon, which causes the page to fill the width of the screen, and then click the mouse button to zoom back out.

8. Click the Close Print Preview ☒ button to return to the main Word screen.

The Print Dialog Box

The Print dialog box allows you to control how your document prints. The following illustration explains some of the important aspects of the dialog box.

FROM THE KEYBOARD
Ctrl + P to open the Print dialog box

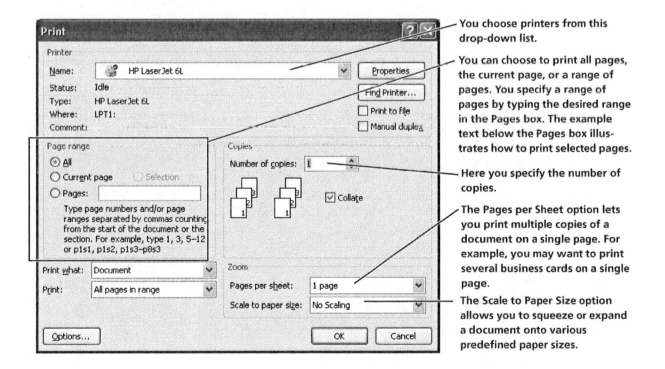

You choose printers from this drop-down list.

You can choose to print all pages, the current page, or a range of pages. You specify a range of pages by typing the desired range in the Pages box. The example text below the Pages box illustrates how to print selected pages.

Here you specify the number of copies.

The Pages per Sheet option lets you print multiple copies of a document on a single page. For example, you may want to print several business cards on a single page.

The Scale to Paper Size option allows you to squeeze or expand a document onto various predefined paper sizes.

Hands-On 2.12   Print the Document

1. Tap ⌈Ctrl⌉+⌈P⌉ to open the Print dialog box.

2. In the Copies area, use the spinner control to specify two copies.

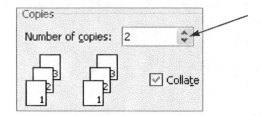

3. Click OK to print two copies of your letter. If your computer is not attached to a local printer, click Cancel to close the Print dialog box.

4. Save 🖫 and close the document.

Concepts Review

True/False Questions

1. The Show/Hide button is used to display nonprinting characters, such as paragraph symbols.   TRUE   FALSE

2. You can select a single word by clicking once on the word.   TRUE   FALSE

3. Before you insert text in a document, you must position the cursor at the point where you want to insert the text.   TRUE   FALSE

4. Word 2007's new line spacing default is 1.5 lines instead of the previous 1.0 line.   TRUE   FALSE

5. Someone using an older version of Word can read your Word 2007 documents by downloading a compatibility pack from the Microsoft website.   TRUE   FALSE

6. The [Backspace] key deletes the character to the right of the cursor.   TRUE   FALSE

7. You use the [Shift] key to select nonadjacent parts of a document.   TRUE   FALSE

8. Holding the [Shift] key while clicking in a sentence selects the entire sentence.   TRUE   FALSE

9. The Clipboard holds up to 24 entries.   TRUE   FALSE

10. The AutoCorrect feature lets you speed up your work by automatically inserting customized text.   TRUE   FALSE

Multiple Choice Questions

1. Which of the following methods can you use to select a paragraph?
   a. Double-click in the paragraph.
   b. Triple-click in the paragraph.
   c. Triple-click anywhere in the left margin.
   d. None of the above

2. Which key should you press if you want to copy while using drag and drop?
   a. [Shift]
   b. [Ctrl]
   c. [Alt]
   d. [Home]

3. Which of the following statements is accurate regarding AutoCorrect?
   a. If AutoCorrect corrects something you do not want corrected, your only option is to delete the corrected term and retype it.
   b. You cannot turn off AutoCorrect.
   c. You cannot delete AutoCorrect entries that come with the Word software.
   d. If Word automatically corrects something that you don't want corrected, an AutoCorrect smart tag option allows you to undo it.

4. Which of the following statements is correct relative to saving a document?
   a. Word 2007 documents are saved in a docQ format.
   b. The Save button is located on the Mini toolbar.
   c. If you are saving a document for the first time, Word displays the Save As dialog box.
   d. You cannot save a Word 2007 document on a USB flash drive.

LESSON 3

Creating a Memorandum and a Press Release

In this lesson, you will expand on the basic Word skills you've developed. You will create a memo and a press release and then apply character formatting. You will also get experience with Word's proofing and editing tools, including Spelling & Grammar check and Find and Replace.

LESSON OBJECTIVES

After studying this lesson, you will be able to:

- Insert dates and symbols
- Insert and delete page breaks
- Work with proofreading tools
- Use character formatting
- Work with Find and Replace

LESSON TIMING

- Concepts/Hands-On: 1 hr 00 min
- Concepts Review: 15 min
- Total: 1 hr 15 min

CASE STUDY: PREPARING A MEMORANDUM

Lashanda Robertson is the public affairs representative for Flexico, Inc., a fabric manufacturer specializing in materials for active wear. Image and public perception are particularly important in the high-profile world of fashion design. Being a savvy company, Flexico understands this, and Lashanda regularly issues press releases to clothing manufacturers and other potential customers, trumpeting forthcoming fabrics and materials. Lashanda creates a memorandum to which she attaches her latest press release announcing the new FlexMax line of fabrics for active wear. Memorandums are used for internal communication within a company or organization, whereas business letters are used for external communication.

Additional learning resources are available at labpub.com/learn/word07_fastcourse1/

Typing a Memorandum

There are a variety of acceptable memorandum styles in use today. All memorandum styles contain the same elements but with varied formatting. The style shown in the following figure is a traditional memorandum style with minimal formatting.

The introduction includes leads such as MEMO TO: and FROM:. Use a double space between paragraphs, or use the new Microsoft spacing, which automatically adds space after a paragraph. This means you only need to tap `Enter` once between paragraphs.

The body of the memo comes next.

Extras such as attachment notations go here.

MEMO TO:	Bill Watson
FROM:	Lashanda Robertson
DATE:	February 10, 2007
SUBJECT:	Flexico Press Release

I have attached a press release to announce the launch of our new FlexMax line of fabrics. Please review the press release and let me know if you have comments or suggestions. I will submit this press release to the media organizations next week.

Attachment

Introducing Tabs

The `Tab` key moves the cursor to the nearest tab stop. In Word, the default tab stops are set every $1/2$ inch, thus the cursor moves $1/2$ inch whenever you tap the `Tab` key. In this lesson, you will use Word's default tab settings. In Lesson 4, Creating a Simple Report, you'll learn to set custom tab stops.

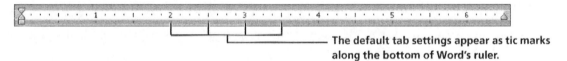

The default tab settings appear as tic marks along the bottom of Word's ruler.

Inserting and Formatting the Date

You use the Insert→Text→Insert Date and Time 🕔 command on the Ribbon to display the Date and Time dialog box. Word lets you insert the current date in a variety of formats. For example, the date could be inserted as 2/10/07, February 10, 2007, or 10 February 2007.

FROM THE KEYBOARD

`Alt`+`Shift`+`D` to insert a date

The Update Automatically Option

You can insert the date and time as text or as a field. Inserting the date as text has the same effect as typing the date into a document. Fields, however, are updated whenever a document is opened or printed. For example, imagine you create a document on February 10, 2007, and you insert the date as a field. If you open the document the next day, the date will automatically change to February 11, 2007. The date and time are inserted as fields whenever the Update Automatically box is checked, as shown here.

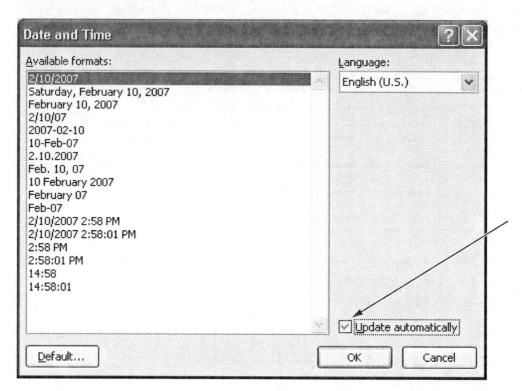

 Hands-On 3.1 **Set Up a Memo and Insert the Date**

1. Start a new blank document. Make sure the Word window is maximized ☐ .

2. If necessary, click the View Ruler ☑ button at the top of the vertical scroll bar to turn on the ruler.

3. Tap ⌊Enter⌋ twice to space down to approximately 2 inches from the top of the page (1-inch mark on the vertical ruler).

4. Type **MEMO TO:** and tap the ⌊Tab⌋ key.

5. If necessary, choose Home→Paragraph→Show/Hide ¶ from the Ribbon to display formatting marks.

6. Type **Bill Watson** and tap ⌊Enter⌋ once.

7. Type **FROM:** and tap ⌊Tab⌋ twice.

8. Type **Lashanda Robertson** and tap ⌊Enter⌋ once.

9. Type **DATE:** and tap ⌊Tab⌋ twice.

10. Choose Insert→Text→Insert Date and Time 🗓 from the Ribbon to display the Date and Time dialog box.

11. Make sure the Update Automatically box is not checked at the bottom of the dialog box.

12. Choose the third date format on the list, and click OK.

13. Complete the remainder of the memorandum, as shown in the following illustration, using the Tab to align the text in the Subject line. Bear in mind that you only need to tap Enter once between paragraphs.

MEMO TO: Bill Watson

FROM: Lashanda Robertson

DATE: February 10, 2007

SUBJECT: Flexico Press Release

I have attached a press release to announce the launch of our new FlexMax line of fabrics. Please review the press release and let me know if you have comments or suggestions. I will submit this press release to the media organizations next week.

Attachment

14. Click the View Ruler button at the top of the scroll bar to turn off the ruler.

15. Choose Home→Paragraph→Show/Hide ¶ from the Ribbon to turn off the formatting marks.

16. Click the Save button, and save the document in Lesson 03 folder as **Robertson Memo**.

17. Leave the memorandum open, as you will modify it throughout this lesson.

Inserting Symbols

Word lets you insert a variety of symbols, typographic characters, and international characters not found on the keyboard. You insert symbols via the Symbol dialog box. The following illustration shows how you access the Symbol dialog box.

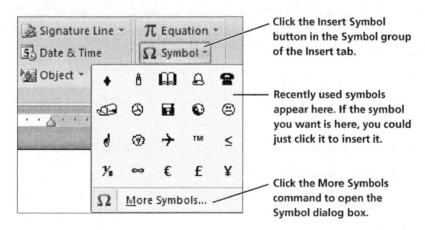

Click the Insert Symbol button in the Symbol group of the Insert tab.

Recently used symbols appear here. If the symbol you want is here, you could just click it to insert it.

Click the More Symbols command to open the Symbol dialog box.

The Special Characters tab displays commonly used special characters, such as the registered trademark ® symbol and various punctuation symbols.

You can choose from several fonts, each displaying a different set of characters in the dialog box. Some fonts, such as Wingdings, contain interesting and fun symbols.

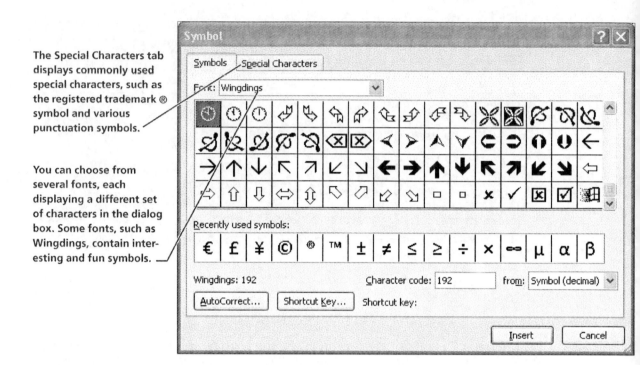

 Hands-On 3.2   Insert Symbols

1. Position the cursor to the right of the word *Flexico* on the *SUBJECT:* line.

2. Click Insert→Symbols→Insert Symbol 𝛀 from the Ribbon, and choose the More Symbols command at the bottom of the menu.

3. When the Symbol dialog box appears, click the Special Characters tab.

4. Choose the registered trademark symbol (an R inside a circle), and then click the Insert button.

5. Position the cursor to the right of *FlexMax* in the main paragraph. (You may need to drag the dialog box out of the way in order to see the word. To do that, position the mouse pointer on the blue title bar at the top of the dialog box, press and hold the mouse button, drag the dialog box out of the way, and then release the mouse button.)

6. Insert the trademark (™) symbol.

7. Click the Symbols tab in the Symbol dialog box, and choose different fonts from the Font list to see other sets of symbols.

8. When you finish experimenting, click the Close button to close the dialog box.

9. Click the Save 🖫 button to save the changes.

Working with Page Breaks

If you are typing text and the cursor reaches the bottom of a page, Word automatically breaks the page and begins a new page. This is known as an automatic page break. The location of automatic page breaks may change as text is added to or deleted from a document. Automatic page breaks are convenient when working with long documents that have continuously flowing text. For example, imagine you were writing a novel and you decided to insert a new paragraph in the middle of a chapter. With automatic page breaks, you could insert the paragraph and Word would automatically repaginate the entire chapter.

You force a page break by choosing Insert→Pages→Page Break ⊟ from the Ribbon. A manual page break remains in place unless you remove it. You insert manual page breaks whenever you want to control the starting point of a new page.

FROM THE KEYBOARD
⌈Ctrl⌉+⌈Enter⌉ to insert
a page break

Removing Manual Page Breaks

In Draft view, a manual page break appears as a horizontal line, including the phrase Page Break. You can also see the page break line in Print Layout view if you turn on the Show/Hide feature. You can remove a manual page break by positioning the cursor on the page break line and tapping ⌈Delete⌉, as shown in the following illustration.

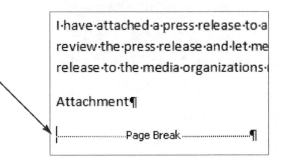

 Hands-On 3.3   Work with Page Breaks

1. Make sure you are in Print Layout view. If you are not sure, click the View tab and choose Print Layout from the Document Views group at the left edge of the Ribbon. (If the button is highlighted, you are already in Print Layout view.)

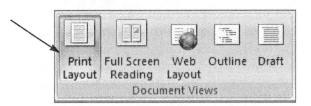

2. Position the cursor at the bottom of the document and, if necessary, tap ⌈Enter⌉ to generate a blank line below the *Attachment* line.

3. Choose Insert→Pages→Page Break ⊟ from the Ribbon.

4. If necessary, scroll down to see the bottom portion of page 1 and the top of page 2.

5. Look at the Status bar at the bottom-left corner of the screen; it shows the page you are on and the total number of pages. (The first number varies, depending on where your cursor is located.) It also displays the number of words in the document.

| Page: 1 of 2 | Words: 61 |

6. Scroll up until the *Attachment* line is visible.

7. If necessary, click Home→Paragraph→Show/Hide ¶ to display formatting marks and see the page break.

8. Click to the left of the page break line, and tap Delete .

9. Try scrolling down to the second page and you will see that it is gone.

10. Check to see that the cursor is just below the *Attachment* line, and tap Ctrl + Enter to reinsert the page break.

11. Click Home→Paragraph→Show/Hide ¶ to hide the formatting marks.

12. Click Office→Open and, if necessary, navigate to your file storage location and open Press Release from the Lesson 03 folder.

13. In the Press Release document, tap Ctrl + A to select the entire document.

14. Tap Ctrl + C to copy the document.

15. On the taskbar, click the Robertson Memo icon to switch back to that document.

16. Make sure your cursor is at the top of page 2.

17. Choose Home→Clipboard→Paste from the Ribbon.

18. Use the taskbar icon to switch to Press Release.

19. Choose Office→Close to close the file.

20. Save the file and leave it open for the next exercise.

Working with Proofreading Tools

Word's powerful Spelling and Grammar tool helps you avoid embarrassing spelling and grammar errors. Whether you choose to use the default on-the-fly checking, where Word marks possible errors as you type, or whether you choose to save proofing tasks until you've completed your document content, these tools can help polish your writing. However, these tools are proofreading aids, not the final word. You still need to involve human judgment in a final round of proofing.

- Spelling checker
- Grammar checker

Using the Spelling Checker

Word checks a document for spelling errors by comparing each word to the contents of a dictionary. Word also looks for double words such as *the the,* and a variety of capitalization errors.

Word can automatically check your spelling as you type. It flags spelling errors by underlining them with wavy red lines. You can correct a flagged error by right-clicking the error and choosing a suggested replacement word or other option from the menu that pops up.

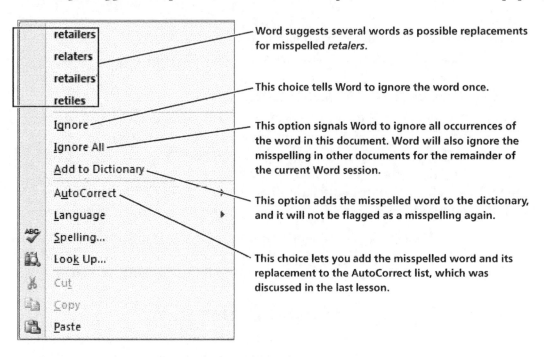

Word suggests several words as possible replacements for misspelled *retalers*.

This choice tells Word to ignore the word once.

This option signals Word to ignore all occurrences of the word in this document. Word will also ignore the misspelling in other documents for the remainder of the current Word session.

This option adds the misspelled word to the dictionary, and it will not be flagged as a misspelling again.

This choice lets you add the misspelled word and its replacement to the AutoCorrect list, which was discussed in the last lesson.

 Hands-On 3.4   Use Automatic Spelling Checker

1. Notice that the word *Flexico* in the first line of page 2 has a wavy red underline. This word appears a number of times in the document.

2. Follow these steps to have the spelling checker ignore all occurrences of *Flexico* and thereby remove the wavy red underline wherever the term appears:

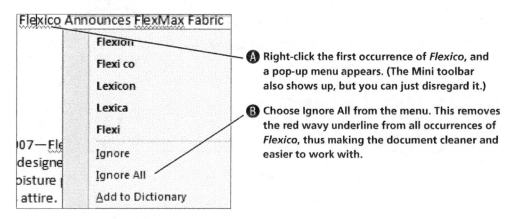

Ⓐ Right-click the first occurrence of *Flexico*, and a pop-up menu appears. (The Mini toolbar also shows up, but you can just disregard it.)

Ⓑ Choose Ignore All from the menu. This removes the red wavy underline from all occurrences of *Flexico*, thus making the document cleaner and easier to work with.

3. Right-click *FlexMax* and choose Ignore All from the pop-up menu.

4. Notice that Word flagged a double word error in the first paragraph of the press release.

5. Right-click the word *for* with the wavy red line, and choose the Delete Repeated Word command from the menu.

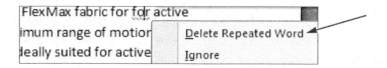

6. Save your file and leave it open for the next exercise.

Using the Grammar Checker

Word has a sophisticated grammar checker that can help you with your writing skills. Like the spelling checker, the grammar checker can check grammar as you type. The grammar checker flags errors by underlining them with wavy green lines. You can correct a flagged error by right-clicking the error and choosing a replacement phrase or other option from the pop-up menu. Be careful when using the grammar checker. It isn't perfect. There is no substitute for careful proofreading.

Grammar checking is active by default. Grammar checking options are available by clicking the Office button, then clicking the Word Options button to display the Word Options window. You can enable or disable the feature by checking or unchecking the boxes.

The Spelling and Grammar Dialog Box

FROM THE KEYBOARD

F7 to start the Spelling & Grammar check

Choose Review→Proofing→Spelling and Grammar from the Ribbon to display the Spelling and Grammar dialog box. You may prefer to focus on your document's content and postpone proofing until you're done. You can use the Spelling and Grammar dialog box for that purpose.

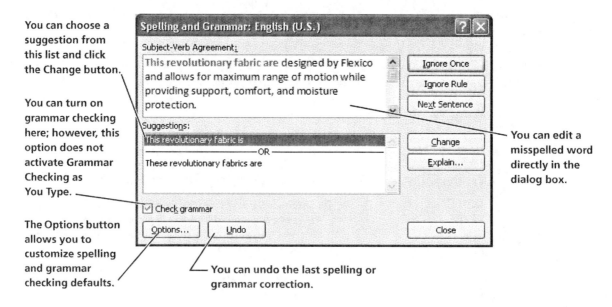

1. Click the Office button, and then click the Word Options button to display the Word Options window.

2. Choose Proofing from the menu on the left.

3. Follow these steps to turn on grammar checking:

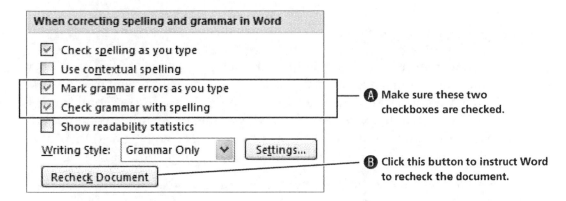

4. When the message box appears, choose Yes to dismiss the message, then click OK to close the window.

5. Position the cursor at the beginning of the first line on page 2.

6. Choose Review→Proofing→Spelling and Grammar ⬛ from the Ribbon.

7. Click the Ignore All button.

8. Click Ignore All again when *FlexMax* appears as a possible spelling error.

9. Follow these steps to correct the grammatical error:

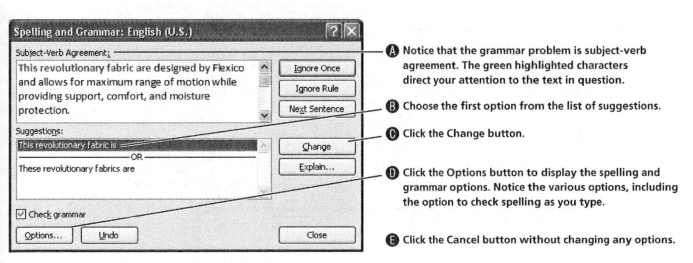

10. The highlighted option *fabric is* in the Suggestions list is the one you want, so click the Change button.

11. The next error is a spelling error, and the suggestion *Delivery* is correct, so click the Change button.

12. Finish checking the rest of the press release using your own good judgment regarding what changes to make. When *Lashanda* is flagged, click the Ignore Once button.

13. When the message appears indicating that the spelling and grammar check is complete, click OK.

14. Save 💾 the file and leave it open for the next exercise.

Formatting Text

FROM THE KEYBOARD
Ctrl + B for bold
Ctrl + U for underline
Ctrl + I for italics

You can format text by changing the font, font size, and color. You can also apply various font formats, including bold, italics, and underline. If you are typing new text and no text is selected, the format settings take effect from the cursor forward or until you change them again. If you wish to format existing text, you must select the text and then apply the desired formats. You can format text using options in the Font dialog box. Display the Font dialog box by clicking the Dialog Box Launcher in the Font group of the Home tab.

The following illustration describes the Font dialog box.

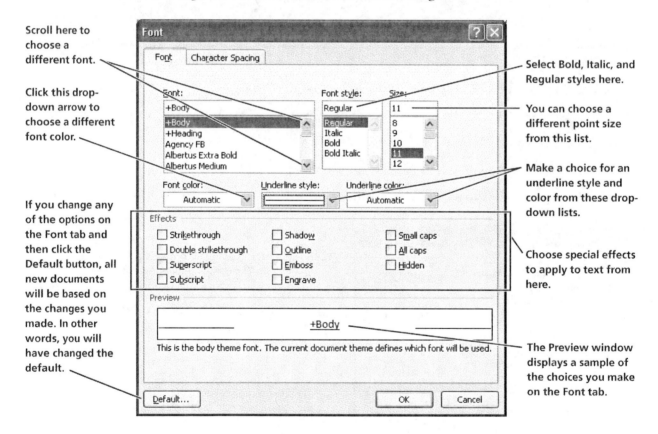

Scroll here to choose a different font.

Click this drop-down arrow to choose a different font color.

If you change any of the options on the Font tab and then click the Default button, all new documents will be based on the changes you made. In other words, you will have changed the default.

Select Bold, Italic, and Regular styles here.

You can choose a different point size from this list.

Make a choice for an underline style and color from these drop-down lists.

Choose special effects to apply to text from here.

The Preview window displays a sample of the choices you make on the Font tab.

Working with Fonts and Themes

All Word 2007 documents are based on a document theme, which is a set of formatting selections including colors, graphic elements, and fonts, all designed to blend well together. There are various themes you can apply to your documents, and the fonts vary depending on the theme.

The theme-related font choices include two fonts, one for body text and one for headings. That's what the first two entries in the Font list of the Font dialog box represent. This dialog box displays the current theme fonts using the generic +Body and +Heading names. You'll also find the theme fonts for the body and headings at the top of the Font drop-down menu in the Font group of the Home tab. Here they display the actual names of the fonts for the current theme. You'll learn more about themes in *FastCourse Word 2007: Level 2.*

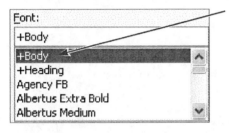

Font list in the Font dialog box

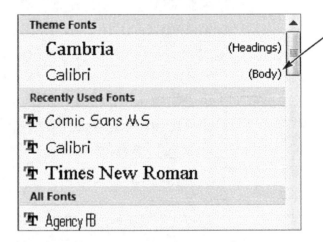

Font list in the Font group on the Home tab

 ## Hands-On 3.6   Format Text

1. Scroll to the top of the second page.

2. Position the mouse pointer in the left margin, and drag down to select the first three heading lines.

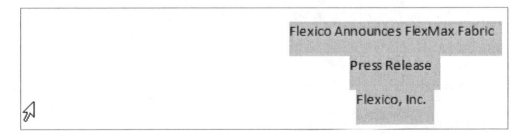

3. Switch to the Home tab on the Ribbon, and then follow these steps to format the lines:

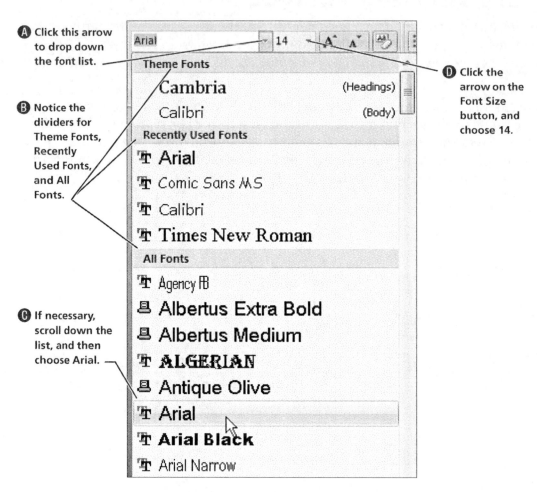

A Click this arrow to drop down the font list.

B Notice the dividers for Theme Fonts, Recently Used Fonts, and All Fonts.

C If necessary, scroll down the list, and then choose Arial.

D Click the arrow on the Font Size button, and choose 14.

4. Make sure the heading lines are still selected. Move the mouse pointer over the selected text. Right-click the selected text to see the toolbar.

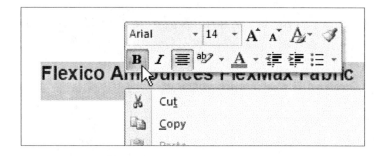

5. Click the Bold **B** button to apply the bold format.

6. Click the Italic **I** button, to apply the format, and then click it again to turn off the italic formatting.

7. Scroll up to the first page of the document to view the memorandum.

8. Click just in front of the word *MEMO* when the mouse pointer is shaped like an I-beam I.

9. Press and hold the ⟨Shift⟩ key, and then tap the ⟨→⟩ key until *MEMO TO:* is selected.

10. Press Ctrl+B to apply bold to the text.

11. Use the techniques in the previous two steps to apply bold to the *FROM:* heading. Remember, select first, and then format.

12. Now apply bold to the other two headings, using the technique of your choice. You may want to try out the Bold command in the Font group of the Home tab.

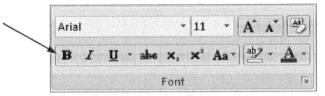

13. Make sure no text is selected, and then click the Dialog Box Launcher in the bottom-right corner of the Font group.

14. Choose Bodoni MT from the Font list, and then click the Default button in the bottom-left corner of the dialog box.

15. When the message box appears asking if you want to change the default font, click Yes.

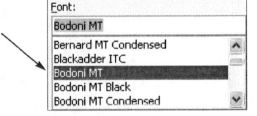

16. Press Ctrl+N to start a new document, and observe the Font list in the Font group.

17. Choose Office→Close to close the blank document.

18. Click the Dialog Box Launcher in the bottom-right corner of the Font group to open the Font dialog box.

19. Make sure the Font tab is in the foreground, and then choose +Body from the top of the list.

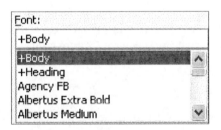

20. Click the Default button, and when the message appears asking if you want to change the default font, click Yes.

21. Save your file and leave it open for the next exercise.

The Format Painter

The Format Painter lets you copy text formats from one location to another. This is convenient if you want the same format(s) applied to text in different locations. The Format Painter copies all text formats, including the font, font size, and color. This saves time and helps create consistent formatting throughout a document. The Format Painter is located in the Clipboard group on the Home tab, and it also appears on the Mini toolbar.

1. Scroll to page 2, and select the heading *Announcement* just above the first large paragraph of text.

2. When the Mini toolbar appears, follow these steps to apply color to the heading line.

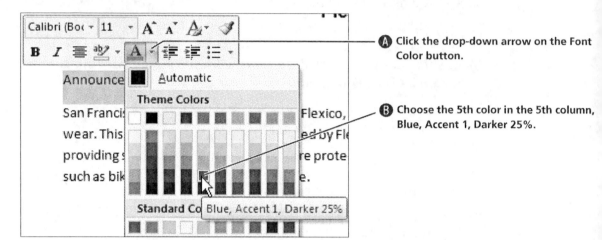

Ⓐ Click the drop-down arrow on the Font Color button.

Ⓑ Choose the 5th color in the 5th column, Blue, Accent 1, Darker 25%.

3. Keep the text selected and the Mini toolbar active, and follow these steps to apply additional formats to the text:

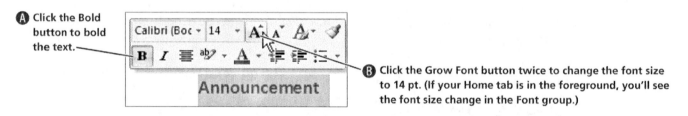

Ⓐ Click the Bold button to bold the text.

Ⓑ Click the Grow Font button twice to change the font size to 14 pt. (If your Home tab is in the foreground, you'll see the font size change in the Font group.)

4. Make sure the heading *Announcement* is selected.

5. Click the Format Painter 🖌 button on the Mini toolbar.

6. Drag the mouse pointer across the *Delivery and Availability* heading, and then release the mouse button.

7. Scroll down so you can see the last two headings on the page.

8. Make sure the *Delivery and Availability* heading is still selected.

9. Double-click the Format Painter.

10. Select the heading *FlexMax Styles* by either dragging the mouse over it or by clicking in front of it in the margin when the mouse pointer is a white arrow.

11. Select the heading *About Flexico* to copy the format to that heading.

12. Choose Home→Clipboard→Format Painter 🖌 to turn it off.

13. Save 🖫 your file and leave it open for the next exercise.

Working with Find and Replace

Word's Find command lets you search a document for a particular word or phrase. You can also search for text formats, page breaks, and a variety of other items. Find is often the quickest way to locate a phrase, format, or item in a document. The Replace option lets you replace the found phrase, format, or item. The Find and Replace commands appear in the Editing group at the right end of the Home tab. Choosing these commands displays the Find and Replace dialog box.

The Find tab provides a text box where you can enter the term you are searching for.

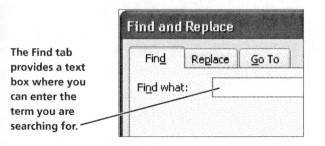

The Replace tab contains two text boxes, one for the Find What term and one for the Replace With term.

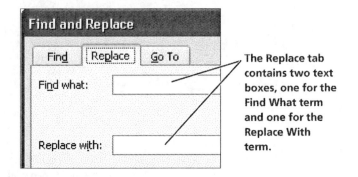

Notice that the Find and Replace tabs appear within the same dialog box.

You type the term you are searching for here.

Click this button if it is labeled More. (The button name toggles between More and Less.) Clicking More displays the bottom half of the dialog box. Clicking Less closes the bottom half.

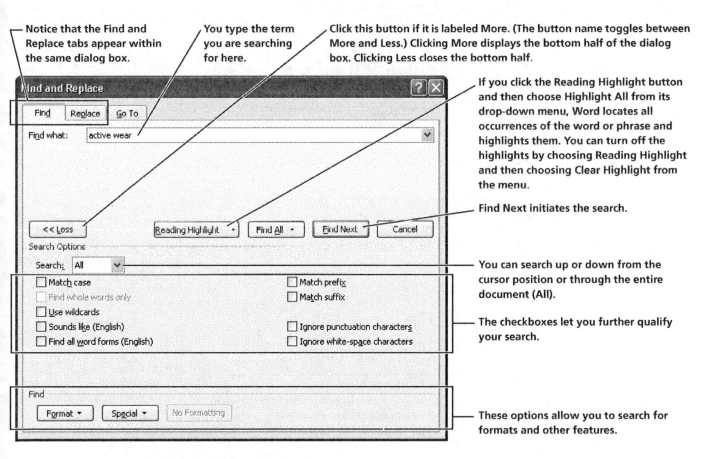

If you click the Reading Highlight button and then choose Highlight All from its drop-down menu, Word locates all occurrences of the word or phrase and highlights them. You can turn off the highlights by choosing Reading Highlight and then choosing Clear Highlight from the menu.

Find Next initiates the search.

You can search up or down from the cursor position or through the entire document (All).

The checkboxes let you further qualify your search.

These options allow you to search for formats and other features.

Finding and Replacing Formats

You may want to replace the formats in a document. Perhaps you formatted certain elements with a particular font and now you want to use a different font. Find and Replace finds the formatted elements for you and automatically replaces them.

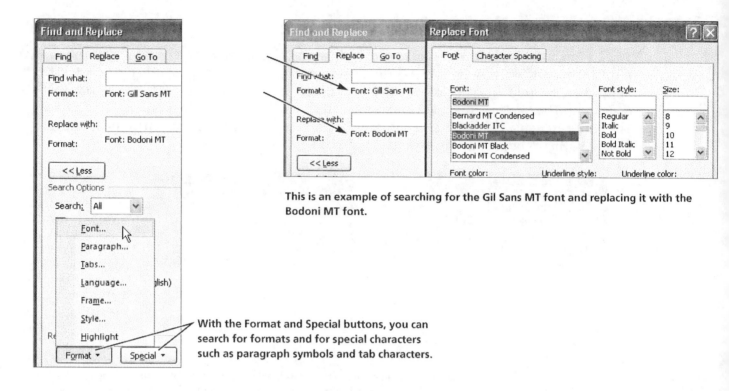

This is an example of searching for the Gil Sans MT font and replacing it with the Bodoni MT font.

With the Format and Special buttons, you can search for formats and for special characters such as paragraph symbols and tab characters.

 Hands-On 3.8   Use Find and Replace

1. Position the cursor at the top of page 2, and make sure no text is selected.

2. Choose Home→Editing→Find 🔍 .

3. Follow these steps to highlight all occurrences of *active wear:*

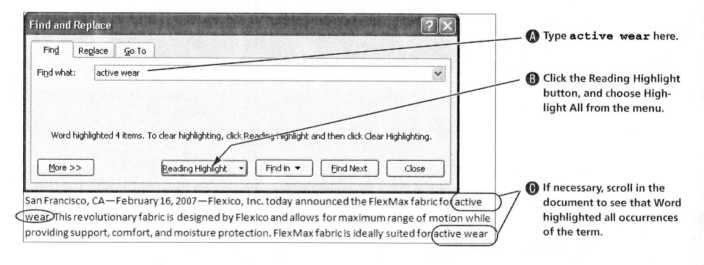

Ⓐ Type **active wear** here.

Ⓑ Click the Reading Highlight button, and choose High-light All from the menu.

Ⓒ If necessary, scroll in the document to see that Word highlighted all occurrences of the term.

4. Click the Reading Highlight button again, and choose Clear Highlighting from the menu.

5. Scroll to the top of the document, and position the cursor anywhere in the first line of the memo.

6. Click in the Find What box, delete *active wear,* and type **Announce** (capital *A*) in its place.

7. Click the Find Next button and Word locates *announce* in the first paragraph of the memo.

8. Click Find Next again and *Announces* is highlighted in the first heading line of the press release.

9. Click the More button in the Find and Replace dialog box to open the bottom section of the dialog box.

10. Click the Match Case checkbox under Search Options.

11. Click the Find Next button, and Word locates the capitalized word *Announcement*.

12. Click Find Next again, and Word indicates that the entire document has been searched.

13. Click OK in the message box.

14. Uncheck the Match Case checkbox.

15. If necessary, scroll to the top of the document, and place the cursor anywhere in the first line of the memo.

16. Check the Find Whole Words Only checkbox.

17. Click Find Next twice, and on the second click Word indicates that the entire document was searched.

18. Click OK in the message box, and then uncheck the Find Whole Words Only checkbox.

19. Delete the word *Announce* in the Find What box.

20. Click the Format button at the bottom of the dialog box.

21. Choose Font from the list.

22. Choose Bold from the Font Style list, and click OK.

23. Click the Find Next button, and Word selects a bolded word.

24. Click the Less button to collapse the bottom portion of the dialog box, and then click the Close button to close the dialog box.

25. Position the cursor at the top of the document, and make sure no text is selected.

26. Press Ctrl+H to display the Find and Replace dialog box.

27. Click the More button to expand the dialog box, and then click the No Formatting button at the bottom of the dialog box.

28. Click the Less button to collapse the dialog box.

29. Type **FlexMax** in the Find What box, and then type **MaxFlex** in the Replace With box.

30. Click the Find Next button to locate the first occurrence of FlexMax.

31. Click the Replace button to make the replacement.

32. Click the Replace All button to make all the changes at once.

33. Click OK to dismiss the message, and then close the Find and Replace dialog box and observe the *MaxFlex* replacements.

34. Save the file and close it.

Concepts Review

True/False Questions

1. You use [Ctrl]+[S] to access the Symbol dialog box.   TRUE   FALSE

2. The Date and Time dialog box allows you to insert the date as text but not as a field.   TRUE   FALSE

3. Using the Font tab in the Font dialog box, you can modify the font, font style, font   TRUE   FALSE
   size, and change the default font.

4. The Format Painter is used to copy and paste formatted text.   TRUE   FALSE

5. Manual page breaks remain in place until you remove them.   TRUE   FALSE

6. Default tab settings are represented as small triangles at the bottom of the ruler.   TRUE   FALSE

7. Word marks a possible grammatical error with a wavy green line.   TRUE   FALSE

8. You only need to tap [Enter] once between paragraphs when using Word's new   TRUE   FALSE
   spacing, which automatically adds space after a paragraph.

9. You can remove a manual page break by clicking it and tapping [Delete].   TRUE   FALSE

10. The +Body and +Heading fonts in the Font dialog box represent the body font and   TRUE   FALSE
    heading font for the current theme a document is based on.

Multiple Choice Questions

1. When you choose Ignore All from the pop-up menu during a spelling check, it means that _____.

   a. Word will ignore all spelling errors for the rest of the document

   b. grammar checking will be ignored until you manually start it again

   c. Word will ignore all occurrences of the word on which you right-clicked

   d. Word will ignore all repeated words

2. To copy text formats to several locations in a document, you select the text containing the formats you want to copy, and then _____.

   a. click the Format Painter button and select the desired blocks of text

   b. double-click the Format Painter button and select the desired blocks of text

   c. use the Copy button

   d. double-click the Copy button.

3. Which shortcut keystrokes do you use to create a manual page break?

   a. [Ctrl]+[Enter]

   b. [Ctrl]+[Spacebar]

   c. [Ctrl]+[Shift]+[Enter]

   d. [Alt]+[Enter]

4. Which of the following statements is true about the Find and Replace feature?

   a. Find does not search for text formats.

   b. The Find and Replace features are located in the Editing group on the Review tab.

   c. You can highlight all occurrences of a word or phrase in a document.

   d. You cannot search for phrases; you must search for one word at a time.

Creating a Simple Report

In this lesson, you will create a simple report. Reports are important documents often used in business and education. You will format your report using various paragraph formatting techniques. Paragraphs are a fundamental part of any Word document. You will learn how to use paragraph alignment techniques, change line spacing, set custom tab stops, and work with Word's indent features. In addition, you will work with bulleted and numbered lists and borders and shading.

LESSON OBJECTIVES

After studying this lesson, you will be able to:

- Create appropriate report formats
- Use paragraph alignment settings
- Set custom line spacing
- Use paragraph indents
- Set custom tab stops
- Use bullets and numbering
- Apply borders and shading
- Insert page numbers

LESSON TIMING

- Concepts/Hands-On: 1 hr 15 min
- Concepts Review: 15 min
- Total: 1 hr 30 min

CASE STUDY: FORMATTING A RESEARCH PAPER

Bill Nelson is a freshman at West Side Junior College. He is enrolled in an information systems course in which Office 2007 is an important component. Bill has been assigned the task of preparing a report on the importance of computer technology in the 21st century. Professor Williams asked Bill to use Word 2007. After conducting the necessary research, Bill uses the paragraph formatting techniques in Word 2007 to prepare a report that is easy to read, properly formatted, and professional in appearance.

Formatting Reports

There are a variety of acceptable report formats. The following example shows a traditional business report in unbound format. Different report formats can be used for research papers and other types of documents.

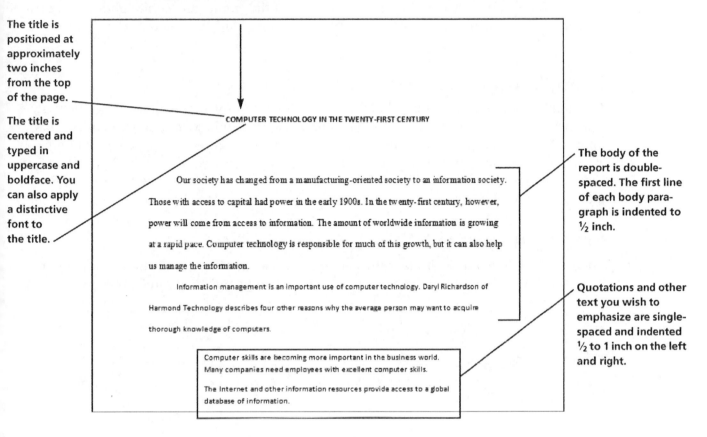

The title is positioned at approximately two inches from the top of the page.

The title is centered and typed in uppercase and boldface. You can also apply a distinctive font to the title.

COMPUTER TECHNOLOGY IN THE TWENTY-FIRST CENTURY

Our society has changed from a manufacturing-oriented society to an information society. Those with access to capital had power in the early 1900s. In the twenty-first century, however, power will come from access to information. The amount of worldwide information is growing at a rapid pace. Computer technology is responsible for much of this growth, but it can also help us manage the information.

Information management is an important use of computer technology. Daryl Richardson of Harmond Technology describes four other reasons why the average person may want to acquire thorough knowledge of computers.

Computer skills are becoming more important in the business world. Many companies need employees with excellent computer skills.

The Internet and other information resources provide access to a global database of information.

The body of the report is double-spaced. The first line of each body paragraph is indented to ½ inch.

Quotations and other text you wish to emphasize are single-spaced and indented ½ to 1 inch on the left and right.

Using Paragraph Formatting

Paragraph formatting includes paragraph alignment, line spacing, paragraph space settings, and bullets and numbering, to mention a few options.

Selecting paragraphs for formatting purposes is a little different from selecting characters. With character formatting, you select the entire block of text you want to format. In the majority of situations this is necessary. With paragraph formatting, you need only click in the paragraph to *select* it. You can highlight the entire paragraph if you wish, but that is not necessary. On the other hand, if you want to apply formatting to more than one paragraph, you must select at least part of each paragraph.

Paragraph Defined

In Word, a paragraph is created anytime you tap the [Enter] key. In other words, a paragraph could consist of several lines that end with an [Enter] or just one line, such as a heading, that ends with an [Enter]. Tapping [Enter] to generate a blank line creates a paragraph, even though there is no text in it. What's more, Word stores formats in the paragraph mark.

Paragraph Formatting Compared to Character Formatting

You use character formatting when you wish to format individual words or a selected block of text. Paragraph formatting affects the entire paragraph.

Character formats are available in the Font group of the Home tab on the Ribbon, while paragraph formats appear in the Paragraph group of the Home tab. Paragraph formats include paragraph alignment, line spacing, borders and shading, bullets and numbering, and indents and tabs.

Using Paragraph Alignment

Paragraph alignment determines how text aligns between the margins. Left alignment gives the paragraph a straight left margin and a ragged right margin. Center alignment is usually applied to headings. Right alignment generates a straight right and a ragged left margin. Justify provides straight left and right margins. You can use several tools to align paragraphs, including the alignment commands in the Paragraph group on the Home tab, the Paragraph dialog box, and the Mini toolbar.

Setting Alignments

The following illustration displays the paragraph alignment commands in the Paragraph group of the Home tab. The Center command is also conveniently located on the Mini toolbar.

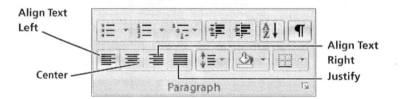

Examples

The following illustration shows how the different paragraph alignment settings look in Word.

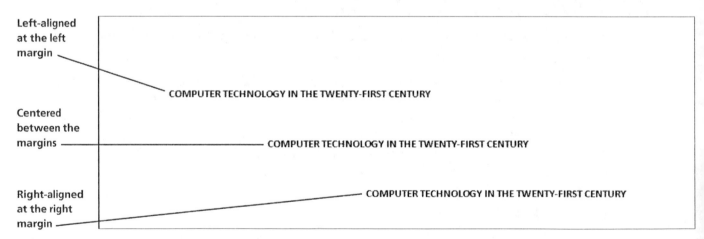

Hands-On 4.1   **Align Text with the Ribbon and Mini Toolbar**

1. Start a blank document, and make sure the Word window is maximized .

2. If necessary, choose View→Document Views→Print Layout to switch to Print Layout view.

3. If the ruler does not appear on the screen, click the View Ruler button at the top of the scroll bar.

4. Tap Enter enough times to position the cursor approximately 2 inches from the top of the page.

5. Turn on Caps Lock and choose Home→Font→Bold **B** from the Ribbon.

6. Type the report title, **COMPUTER TECHNOLOGY IN THE TWENTY-FIRST CENTURY**.

7. Turn off Bold and Caps Lock, and then tap Enter twice.

8. Position the cursor in the report heading.

9. Choose Home→Paragraph→Center from the Ribbon.

10. Choose Home→Paragraph→Align Text Right from the Ribbon.

11. Choose Home→Paragraph→Align Text Left from the Ribbon.

12. Right-click on the heading to display the Mini toolbar.

13. Click the Center button on the toolbar to center the heading.

14. Save the file in the Lesson 04 folder as **Computer Report**, leave the file open, and continue with the next topic.

Setting Line Spacing

2007 new!

The Line Spacing button in the Paragraph group of the Home tab lets you set line spacing for one or more paragraphs. Word 2007's default line spacing is 1.15. You apply line spacing by selecting the desired paragraph(s) and choosing the desired line spacing from the Line Spacing drop-down list.

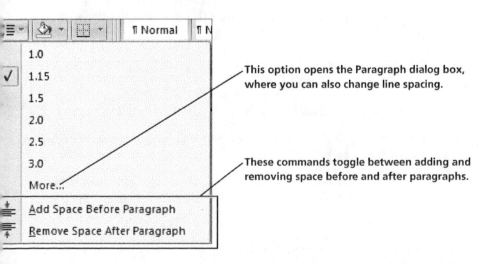

This option opens the Paragraph dialog box, where you can also change line spacing.

These commands toggle between adding and removing space before and after paragraphs.

FROM THE KEYBOARD

Ctrl+1 for single spacing
Ctrl+1.5 for 1.5 spacing
Ctrl+2 for double spacing

1. If necessary, choose Home→Paragraph→Show/Hide ¶ to display formatting characters.

2. Position the cursor on the second paragraph symbol below the title.

3. Choose Home→Paragraph→Line Spacing ⬍☰ from the Ribbon, and click 2.0 for double-spacing.

4. Tap the [Tab] key once to create a $1/2$-inch indent at the start of the paragraph.

5. Now type the following paragraph, but only tap [Enter] once after the last line in the paragraph, since double-spacing is in effect.

> Our society has changed from a manufacturing-oriented society to an information society. Those with access to capital had power in the early 1900s. In the twenty-first century, however, power will come from access to information. The amount of worldwide information is growing at a rapid pace. Computer technology is responsible for much of this growth, but it can also help us manage the information.

6. Make sure you tap [Enter] after the last line. Tap [Tab] once, and type the following paragraph.

> Information management is an important use of computer technology. Daryl Richardson of Harmond Technology describes four other reasons why the average person may want to acquire thorough knowledge of computers.

7. Tap [Enter] to complete the paragraph, and then press [Ctrl]+[1] (use the [1] in the number row, not the number pad) to set single-spacing.

8. Now type the following paragraphs, tapping [Enter] between paragraphs. You don't need to tap [Enter] twice because of the default additional spacing after paragraphs. Do not tab at the beginning of these paragraphs.

> Computer skills are becoming more important in the business world. Many companies need employees with excellent computer skills.
>
> The Internet and other information resources provide access to a global database of information.
>
> Computer skills can often simplify one's personal life. Computers can be used to entertain, to manage finances, and to provide stimulating learning exercises for children.
>
> Using computers can provide a sense of accomplishment. Many people suffer from "computerphobia." Learning to use computers often creates a feeling of connection with the information age.

9. Save your document, and continue with the next topic.

Indenting Text

Indenting offsets text from the margins. The left indent is the most widely used, offsetting lines from the left margin. Likewise, the right indent sets off all lines from the right margin. The first-line indent sets off just the first line of paragraphs. This is similar to using Tab at the start of a paragraph. The hanging indent sets off all lines except for the first line.

Adjusting Indent Settings

The Increase Indent 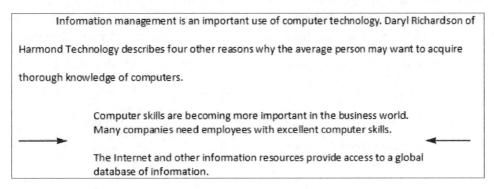 and Decrease Indent commands in the Paragraph group of the Home tab let you adjust the left indent. These buttons increase or decrease the left indent to the nearest tab stop. Word's default tab stops are set every $1/2$ inch, so the left indent changes $1/2$ inch each time you click either command. You can also set indents by using the Paragraph dialog box or by dragging indent markers on the horizontal ruler.

Information management is an important use of computer technology. Daryl Richardson of Harmond Technology describes four other reasons why the average person may want to acquire thorough knowledge of computers.

Computer skills are becoming more important in the business world. Many companies need employees with excellent computer skills.

The Internet and other information resources provide access to a global database of information.

These paragraphs are indented 1 inch from the left and right margins.

 Hands-On 4.3   Experiment with Left Indents

1. Click in one of the single-spaced paragraphs you just typed.

2. Choose Home→Paragraph→Increase Indent from the Ribbon.

3. Choose Home→Paragraph→Decrease Indent from the Ribbon to remove the indent.

4. Use the mouse to select any part of two or more paragraphs.

5. Choose Home→Paragraph→Increase Indent twice to create a 1-inch left indent on each of the selected paragraphs.

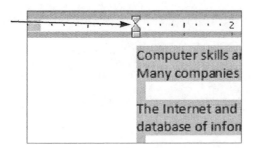

6. Now click Decrease Indent twice to remove the indents.

7. Save the file. You will continue to work with indents in the next exercise.

Setting Custom Indents on the Ruler

You can set indents by dragging the indent markers on the horizontal ruler. The following illustration shows the ruler and the indent markers.

Indent Markers

The indent markers at the left edge of the ruler are made up of two pieces: a top piece and a bottom piece (see the following illustration). You can drag these two pieces independently of each other. The top piece controls the first line of the paragraph when you drag it to the left or right. The bottom piece is a little trickier. It is made up of two sections, but the sections do not come apart. The bottom piece functions differently, depending on whether you place the tip of the mouse in the triangle or the rectangle. Dragging the bottom triangle affects the *rest* of the paragraph (everything but the first line). Dragging the rectangle affects *both triangles*, positioning the first line and all subsequent lines of the paragraph simultaneously.

You use the indent marker at the right end of the ruler to indent the paragraph from the right.

Indents the first line of a paragraph. Makes a hanging indent (see note below). Indents all lines of a paragraph from the left.

 Indents all lines of the paragraph from the right.

Hands-On 4.4 Use the Indent Marker to Indent Paragraphs

1. Select all four single-spaced paragraphs at the bottom of the document.

2. Follow these steps to adjust the left and right indents:

Ⓐ Position the mouse pointer on the Left Indent marker (the bottom rectangle).

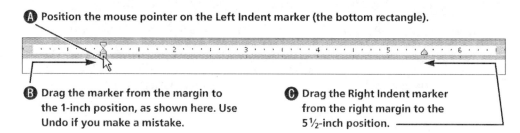

Ⓑ Drag the marker from the margin to the 1-inch position, as shown here. Use Undo if you make a mistake.

Ⓒ Drag the Right Indent marker from the right margin to the 5½-inch position.

3. Position the cursor anywhere in the paragraph beginning *Computer skills can often....*

4. Position the mouse pointer on the First Line Indent marker (the top triangle), and drag it to the right to the $1^1/_2$-inch mark on the ruler.

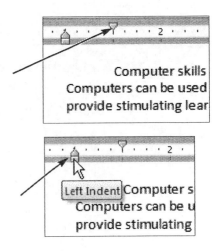

5. Position the mouse pointer in the Left Indent marker (rectangle), and drag it to the right to the $1^1/_2$-inch mark on the ruler.

6. Place the mouse pointer in the top triangle, and drag it left to the $1^1/_2$-inch mark.

7. Feel free to experiment with the indent markers.

8. When you finish, place both pieces of the left markers at the 1-inch position and the Right Indent marker at $5^1/_2$ inches, as shown in the following illustration.

9. Save the file, and leave it open for the next exercise.

Using Custom Tab Stops

Default tab stops are set every $^1/_2$ inch, so the cursor moves $^1/_2$ inch whenever you tap the `Tab` key. You can change the default tab stops if you want the cursor to move a smaller or larger distance when you tap `Tab` or when you want to use a special tab, such as a center tab or a right-align tab. You should always avoid using the `Spacebar` to line up columns of text. Columns may go out of alignment if you decide to change fonts or edit the text. Custom tab stops are also useful for creating leader lines. The dots you see in a table of contents leading to the page numbers are an example of leader lines.

Setting Custom Tab Stops with the Ruler

Word provides four types of custom tab stops: left, right, center, and decimal. You can set all four types using the horizontal ruler. You set tabs by choosing the desired tab type from the Tabs box at the left end of the ruler. Then you click at the desired location on the ruler to set the tab. The tab is set for the paragraph containing the cursor or for all selected paragraphs. You can move a custom tab stop by dragging it to a different location on the ruler.

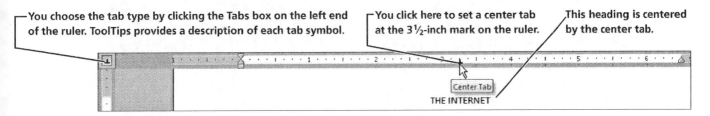

┌ You choose the tab type by clicking the Tabs box on the left end of the ruler. ToolTips provides a description of each tab symbol.   ┌ You click here to set a center tab at the $3^1/_2$-inch mark on the ruler.   ┌ This heading is centered by the center tab.

1. Move the cursor to the bottom of the page and, if necessary, tap [Enter] to generate a blank line at the bottom of the document.

2. Tap [Ctrl]+[Enter] to insert a page break.

3. Set the left and right indent markers at the margins, as shown here.

4. Choose Home→Paragraph→Show/Hide [¶] from the Ribbon to turn on formatting marks.

5. Select the paragraph symbol at the top of page 2.

6. Choose Home→Paragraph→Line Spacing [≣] from the Ribbon, and choose Remove Space After Paragraph from the menu.

7. Choose Home→Paragraph→Show/Hide [¶] from the Ribbon to turn off formatting marks.

8. Follow these steps to set and use a center tab:

Ⓐ Click this box until the Center Tab symbol appears, as shown here. Hover the mouse pointer over the tab symbol to display a ToolTip to verify that you selected the Center Tab.

Ⓑ Click just under the 3¼-inch tic mark on the ruler to set a center tab; 3¼ inches is the center of the line.

Center Tab
THE INTERNET

Ⓒ Tap the [Tab] key, and the cursor moves to the 3¼-inch mark.

Ⓓ Turn on [Caps Lock] and type **THE INTERNET**, and then turn off [Caps Lock].

9. Tap [Enter] twice.

10. Save your file, and leave it open for the next exercise.

Working with the Tabs Dialog Box

You can also set custom tab stops in the Tabs dialog box. You access the dialog box by clicking the Dialog Box Launcher in the Paragraph group of the Home tab and then clicking the Tabs button. In the dialog box, you can specify precise positions for custom tabs, clear custom tab stops, and set leader tabs.

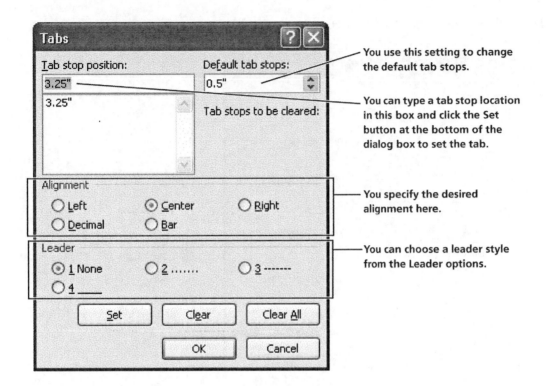

You use this setting to change the default tab stops.

You can type a tab stop location in this box and click the Set button at the bottom of the dialog box to set the tab.

You specify the desired alignment here.

You can choose a leader style from the Leader options.

 Hands-On 4.6   Use the Tabs Dialog Box

1. Make sure the cursor is in the second line below the heading line.

2. Click the Dialog Box Launcher ▣ in the bottom-right corner of the Paragraph group on the Home tab.

3. When the Paragraph dialog box appears, click the Tabs button in the bottom-left corner to display the Tabs dialog box.

4. Click the Clear All button to remove the custom tab stop from the Tab Stop Position list.

5. Click OK, and the tab symbol disappears from the ruler.

6. Type **An Evolution and a Revolution**, and then tap ⌑Enter⌑.

7. Type the following paragraph:

> The Internet is largely responsible for the information explosion we see today. Many people and organizations contributed to its development over many years. The following table shows some high points in the evolution of the Internet.

8. Tap ⌑Enter⌑ twice, and then click the Dialog Box Launcher ▣ in the bottom-right corner of the Paragraph group on the Home tab.

9. When the Paragraph dialog box appears, click the Tabs button in the bottom-left corner to display the Tabs dialog box.

10. Follow these steps to set three left tabs:

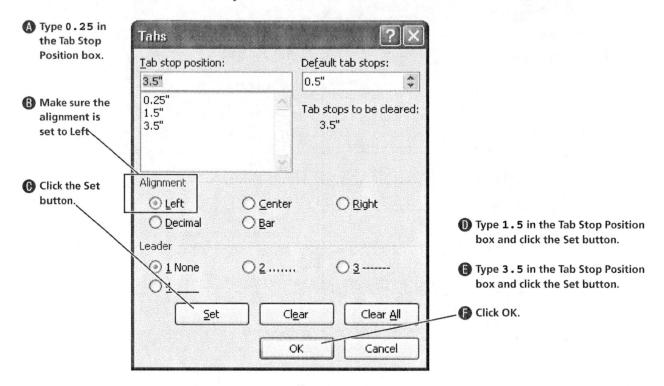

Ⓐ Type 0.25 in the Tab Stop Position box.

Ⓑ Make sure the alignment is set to Left.

Ⓒ Click the Set button.

Ⓓ Type 1.5 in the Tab Stop Position box and click the Set button.

Ⓔ Type 3.5 in the Tab Stop Position box and click the Set button.

Ⓕ Click OK.

11. Tap the Tab key and type **Year.**

12. Tap Tab and type **Event.**

13. Tap Tab and type **Responsible Person/Agency,** and then tap Enter.

14. Tap Tab to align the cursor below *Year.*

15. Continue typing and tabbing to create the text as shown in the following illustration. Remember to tap Tab at the beginning of each line.

Year	Event	Responsible Person/Agency
1969	ARPAnet	Advanced Research Projects Agency
1970s	Backbone is built	National Science Foundation
1989	WWW proposal	Tim Berners-Lee at CERN
1993	First graphical browser	Marc Andreesen leads NCSA team
1994	Netscape is born	Marc Andreesen and Jim Clark

16. When you finish, apply Bold **B** to the heading of the table.

17. Save your file, but leave it open for the next exercise.

Modifying Tab Stops with the Ruler

To adjust a tab setting on the ruler, you select the tabular table and then simply drag the tab symbol to the new location. To delete a tab stop, you just drag the tab symbol off the ruler.

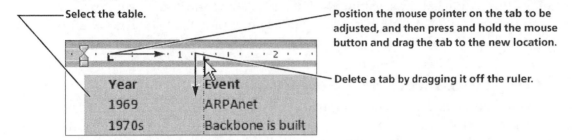

Select the table.

Position the mouse pointer on the tab to be adjusted, and then press and hold the mouse button and drag the tab to the new location.

Delete a tab by dragging it off the ruler.

 Hands-On 4.7   Modify and Delete Tab Stops from the Ruler

1. Select the tabular table.

2. Position the mouse pointer on the tab stop at the $1\frac{1}{2}$-inch position, press and hold the mouse button, and drag to the left to the $1\frac{1}{4}$-inch position, and then release the mouse button.

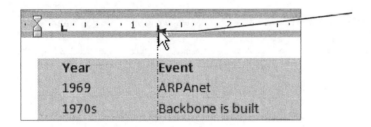

3. Position the cursor at the end of the last line of the table, and tap [Enter] twice.

4. Make sure your cursor is on the second blank line below the table.

5. Position the mouse pointer over the tab symbol at the $\frac{1}{4}$-inch position, and then press and hold the mouse button and drag straight down into the document.

6. Release the mouse button, and the tab is no longer on the ruler.

7. Repeat that process to remove the remaining tabs at $1\frac{1}{4}$ inches and $3\frac{1}{2}$ inches.

8. Save the file but leave it open, as you will use it in the next exercise.

Using Bulleted and Numbered Lists

The Bullets ⬛ and Numbering ⬛ commands in the Paragraph group on the Home tab provide a quick and easy way to create bulleted and numbered lists. You can apply bullets and numbers to existing lists by selecting the list and clicking the desired command. For a new list, you can turn on bullets or numbers when you begin typing the list. Lists are automatically renumbered if items are inserted or deleted.

Turning Off Bullets and Numbering

When you type a list, you should complete the list by tapping Enter after the last paragraph in the list. You can then turn off bullets or numbering for the first line following the list by clicking the Bullets or the Numbering button. Tapping Enter twice also turns off bullets or numbering.

 Hands-On 4.8   **Work with Bullets and Numbering**

1. Make sure the cursor is two lines below the table. Then type the following heading and introductory paragraph:

> Search Engines
> Knowing how to access information on the Internet typically means that you need to be familiar with search engines. Some of the best known search engines include:

2. Tap Enter twice at the end of the paragraph.

3. Choose Home→Paragraph→Bullets ⬛ on the Ribbon.

4. Type **Google** as the first search engine, and then tap Enter to generate the next bullet.

- Google
- AllTheWeb
- Yahoo
- Dogpile
- Ask
- Vivisimo

5. Finish typing the list as shown, tapping Enter after each item to generate the next bullet.

6. Tap Enter three times following the last item in the list to turn off bullets.

7. Type the following heading and introductory paragraph:

> World Wide Web Consortium Goals
> The World Wide Web Consortium (W3C) is an organization that sets standards for developing common protocols that promote the evolution of the Internet and insure cross-platform communications. Below is a listing of their goals and principles.

8. Tap Enter twice at the end of the paragraph.

9. Choose Home→Paragraph→Numbering ⬛ from the Ribbon.

10. Type **Universal Access,** and then tap ⌷Enter⌷ to generate the next number.

11. Complete the list as shown to the right.

12. Tap ⌷Enter⌷ twice following the last item to stop the numbering and generate a blank line.

13. Type **(Bullet point titles taken from http://www.w3.org/Consortium/Points)** to give credit to the W3C website for the list.

14. Save your file, and continue with the next topic.

1.	Universal Access
2.	Semantic Web
3.	Trust
4.	Interoperability
5.	Evolvability
6.	Decentralization
7.	Cooler Multimedia!

Using the Bullets and Numbering Libraries

The arrows ⌷▾⌷ on the Bullets and Numbering buttons provide access to bullets and numbering libraries, where you can choose a style for your bulleted or numbered list or define new formats.

The bullets and numbering libraries shown in the following illustrations display the available built-in styles.

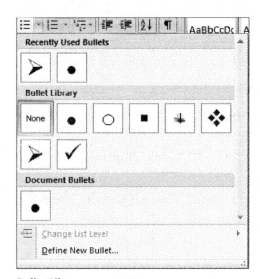

Bullet Library

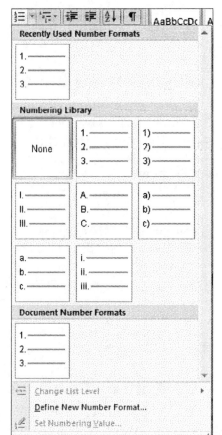

Numbering Library

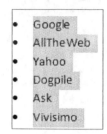

Hands-On 4.9   Change the Bullet Style

1. Select the bulleted list, as shown here.

- Google
- AllTheWeb
- Yahoo
- Dogpile
- Ask
- Vivisimo

2. Click the drop-down arrow on the Bullets ⁝☰ ▾ button and choose the circle bullet.

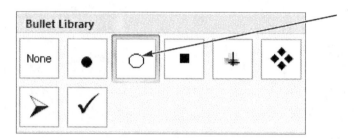

3. Save your file, and leave it open for the next exercise.

Customizing Bullet and Number Styles

You can customize the built-in bullet and number styles. You can define a new bullet or number format by clicking the drop-down arrow on the Bullet or Numbering button and choosing Define New Bullet or Define New Numbering Style.

You can choose from a variety of symbols, pictures, and fonts. ⎯

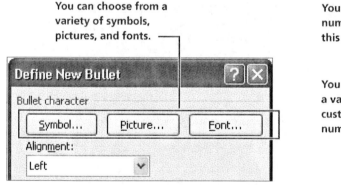

You can select a number style from this list.

You can choose from a variety of fonts to customize your numbering style.

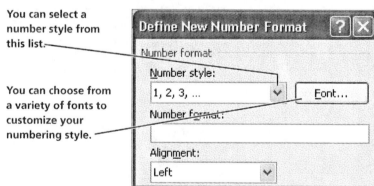

Restart or Continue Numbering

Many documents have more than one numbered list. Sometimes you may want the numbering to continue sequentially from one list to the next. For example, if one list ends with the number 4

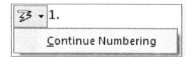

you may want the next list to begin with the number 5. When you begin the next list in your document, Word assumes you want to restart numbering at 1. If you want to continue numbering from the previous list, Word provides an AutoCorrect smart tag when you start additional numbered lists in a document. You can click the AutoCorrect Options smart tag and choose Continue Numbering.

 Hands-On 4.10   Experiment with Custom Bullets

1. Click anywhere in your bulleted list.

2. Choose Home→Paragraph→ Bullets menu ▾ to display the Bullets library, and then choose Define New Bullet from the bottom of the menu.

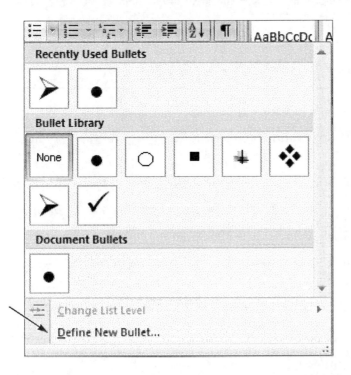

3. When the Define New Bullet dialog box appears, click the Picture button to display the Picture Bullet dialog box.

4. Click the bullet of your choice, and then click OK twice to apply the customized bullet.

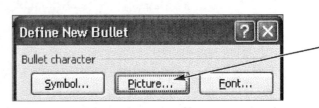

5. Choose Home→Paragraph→ Bullets menu ▾ to display the Bullet library. Notice that your new bullet now appears in the library.

6. Click in the document to close the library.

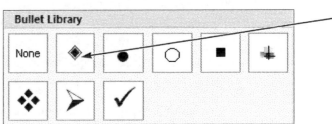

7. Click Undo 🔄 to return the bulleted list to the circle-style bullet.

Setting Line Breaks

When working with bullets and numbering, tapping [Enter] generates a new bullet or number. What if you want to type something relative to a bulleted or numbered item on the next line(s) without generating a new bullet or number? A manual *line break* starts a new line (without inserting a paragraph mark) and continues the text on the new line. The new line is part of the same paragraph as the preceding line. Line breaks are inserted with the [Shift]+[Enter] keystroke combination.

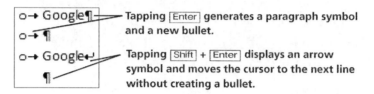

 Hands-On 4.11   **Insert Line Breaks in a List**

1. Place the cursor after *Google* in your bulleted list.

2. Tap [Shift]+[Enter] to generate a line break rather than a paragraph break.

3. If necessary, click the Show/Hide [¶] button to see the line break, which appears as a small arrow at the end of the line. Then click Show/Hide again to turn off formatting marks.

4. Type the following: **This search engine is tops on many people's list**.

5. Click at the end of *AllTheWeb* and tap [Shift]+[Enter] to generate a line break.

6. Type the following: **This search engine provides a highly-relevant hit list**.

7. Use the following illustration to finish adding descriptions to your list:

> o Google
>   The Google search engine is tops on many people's list.
> o AllTheWeb
>   This search engine provides a highly-relevant hit list.
> o Yahoo
>   Yahoo is the oldest directory-type search engine and a favorite of many.
> o Dogpile
>   This search engine stands out in the meta search engine category.
> o Ask
>   Ask claims to have two billion searchable pages.
> o Vivisimo
>   Vivisimo offers unique advanced search techniques.

8. Save your file and leave it open, as you will use it in the next exercise.

Using the Paragraph Space Settings

If you want extra space between paragraphs, you can use Word 2007's default spacing, which automatically adds after-paragraph spacing. The following illustration of the Paragraph group on the Page Layout tab shows the default 10 point after-paragraph spacing. You can use the spinner controls on the Before and After Spacing buttons to adjust the amount of space. You can also use the spacing controls in the Paragraph dialog box in the same way.

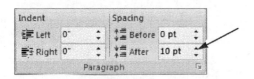 

Paragraph spacing controls in the Paragraph group on the Page Layout tab.

Paragraph spacing controls in the Paragraph dialog box.

Paragraph Spacing Defined

A point (pt) is just 1/72nd of an inch. This fine unit of measure, common in printing, facilitates great precision. Word uses points for type size and other settings, such as paragraph spacing.

 Hands-On 4.12   Set Paragraph Spacing

1. Position the cursor in *An Evolution and a Revolution* toward the top of page 2.

2. Click the Page Layout tab to display its Paragraph group.

3. In the Spacing area, click in the After box and type **4**, and then tap Enter.

4. Place the cursor in the *Search Engines* heading, and then type **4** in the After box and tap Enter.

5. Use the same technique to add 4 points of extra space after the heading *World Wide Web Consortium Goals*.

6. Save the file, and leave it open for the next exercise.

Using Borders and Shading

You can apply borders and shading to selected text, paragraphs, and pages. In this lesson, you will apply borders to paragraphs. Borders can attach to the top, bottom, left, and right edges of paragraphs. You can choose the style, color, and thickness of borders, and you can also select various shading patterns and colors.

The Borders Button

Clicking the menu ▼ button on the borders button in the Paragraph group of the Home tab displays a menu of border options. The Borders and Shading command at the bottom of the menu opens the Borders and Shading dialog box.

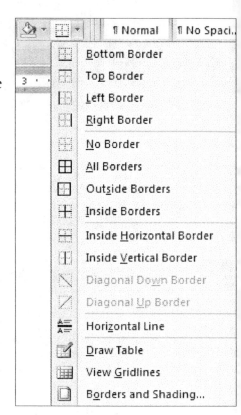

The borders button has a memory. It displays the last choice you made from the menu on the button face. That way you can apply the same type of border several times in a row without opening the menu. The button name changes accordingly.

Example

The border button that appears when you first start Word is named Bottom Border; it looks like this:

If you apply an outside border, as an example, the button is named Outside Border; it looks like this:

The Shading Button

The Shading button 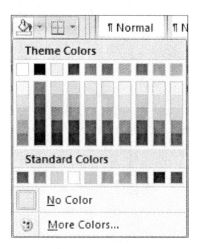 located in the Paragraph group of the Home tab provides a quick way to apply shading.

The Borders and Shading Dialog Box

Choose Borders and Shading from the Borders 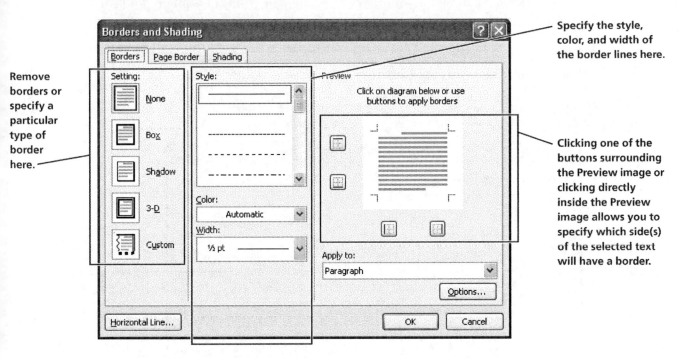 ▾ menu ▾ on the Ribbon to display the dialog box. The following illustrations show the features available in the Borders tab and the Shading tab of the dialog box.

Specify the style, color, and width of the border lines here.

Remove borders or specify a particular type of border here.

Clicking one of the buttons surrounding the Preview image or clicking directly inside the Preview image allows you to specify which side(s) of the selected text will have a border.

Click the Fill color drop-down list to display a gallery of color choices.

Click one of the squares to specify your shading color.

Hands-On 4.13   Apply a Border and Shading to Headings

1. Click anywhere in the line *An Evolution and a Revolution*.

2. Choose Home→Paragraph→Borders ▾ menu ▾ from the Ribbon, and then choose the Borders and Shading command at the bottom of the gallery to display the dialog box.

3. Make sure the Borders tab at the top of the dialog box is in the foreground.

4. Follow these steps to apply a border to the first heading:

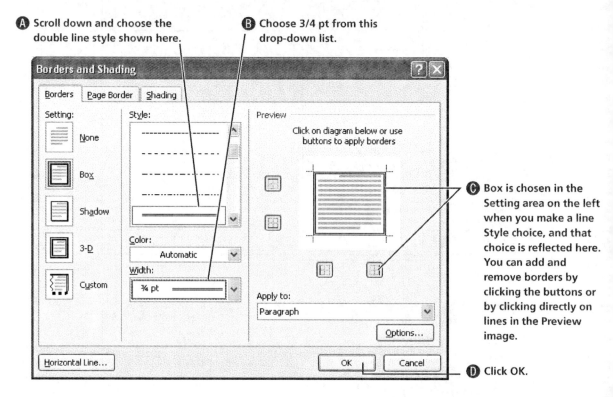

Ⓐ Scroll down and choose the double line style shown here.

Ⓑ Choose 3/4 pt from this drop-down list.

Ⓒ Box is chosen in the Setting area on the left when you make a line Style choice, and that choice is reflected here. You can add and remove borders by clicking the buttons or by clicking directly on lines in the Preview image.

Ⓓ Click OK.

5. Choose Page Layout→Page Background→Page Borders 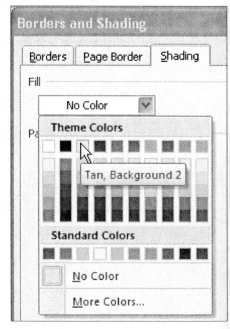 from the Ribbon to display the Borders and Shading dialog box.

6. Click the Shading tab, and then click the Fill color drop-down list.

7. Choose Tan, Background 2 from the list, as shown at right, and then click OK.

8. Make sure your cursor is still in the heading *An Evolution and a Revolution*.

9. Choose Home→Clipboard from the Ribbon.

10. Double-click the Format Painter . Remember, double-clicking keeps the Format Painter turned on.

11. Click in the *Search Engines* heading, and then click in the *World Wide Web Consortium Goals* heading to format the headings.

12. Click Format Painter again to turn it off.

13. Save the file, and leave it open for the next exercise.

Setting Page Numbering

You can insert page numbers at various positions on a page. Page numbering is associated with headers and footers, which you'll learn more about in *FastCourse Word 2007: Level 2*.

A page numbering gallery offers a variety of page numbering designs. Choose Insert→Header & Footer→Page Number from the Ribbon to display a menu of varying positions for your page numbers. Choose a position, and then click the desired style to insert page numbers in your document.

 Hands-On 4.14   Insert Page Numbers

1. Choose Insert→Header & Footer→Page Number from the Ribbon.

2. Follow these steps to insert page numbering:

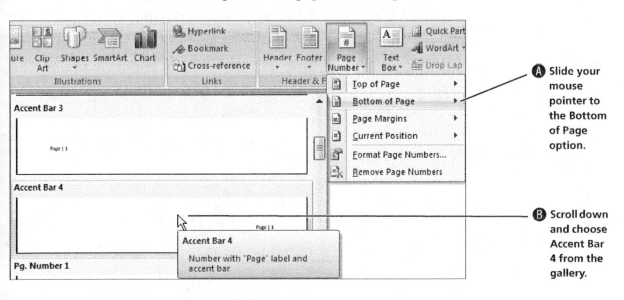

3. Double-click the body of the document to close the footer area.

4. Scroll through the document and observe the page numbering.

5. Save your report and close it.

Concepts Review

True/False Questions

1. When you use paragraph formatting features, you only need to click in the paragraph to select it.   TRUE   FALSE

2. You can set indents by dragging the indent markers on the horizontal ruler.   TRUE   FALSE

3. In Word, the default tab stops are set every $^1/_4$ inch.   TRUE   FALSE

4. Bulleted lists automatically renumber if items are inserted or deleted.   TRUE   FALSE

5. You cannot continue numbering from one list to another within a document.   TRUE   FALSE

6. Only the first line of a paragraph is indented when a hanging indent is applied.   TRUE   FALSE

7. You can remove a custom tab stop by dragging it off the ruler with the mouse pointer.   TRUE   FALSE

8. You can customize the built-in bullets and number styles.   TRUE   FALSE

9. You can use the Mini toolbar to right-align headings in a report.   TRUE   FALSE

10. The Tabs dialog box provides the option to add a leader line to a tab stop.   TRUE   FALSE

Multiple Choice Questions

1. You insert a line break in a bulleted list in order to _____.
   a. generate a new bullet
   b. indent the list
   c. start a new line without generating a bullet
   d. split the list into two separate lists

2. Which of the following items fall in the category of paragraph formatting?
   a. Change line spacing
   b. Change point size
   c. Apply the bold feature
   d. Change to the Cambria (Headings) font

3. Which of the following statements is correct regarding indents?
   a. The Increase Indent command lets you adjust the left and right indents.
   b. Indenting offsets text from the margins.
   c. The bottom triangle on the indent marker is used to modify the first line of a paragraph.
   d. Clicking the Increase Indent button indents the line a $^1/_4$ inch based on Word's default tab settings.

4. Which of the following is an accurate statement about tab stops?
   a. You can set tab leader lines on the ruler.
   b. You cannot modify the position of a tab using the ruler.
   c. You can move a tab by dragging it to a new location on the ruler with the mouse pointer.
   d. You can set a tab by dragging the tab icon from the Tab box onto the ruler.

LESSON 5

Using Mail Merge

In this lesson, you will learn to manage mail using Word 2007's Mail Merge feature. You will set up data sources where you store contact information, and you will set up form letters. Then you'll merge your form letters with a data source to produce personalized letters. You'll also learn to generate personalized envelopes, labels, and other documents.

LESSON OBJECTIVES

After studying this lesson, you will be able to:

- Work with the Mailings tab on the Ribbon
- Work with data sources
- Create main documents
- Conduct a mail merge
- Work with merge problems
- Generate envelopes and mailing labels with Mail Merge

LESSON TIMING

- Concepts/Hands-On:
  1 hr 00 min
- Concepts Review:
  15 min
- Total:
  1 hr 15 min

CASE STUDY: GENERATING A MARKETING MASS MAILING

Linda Adams is the chief executive officer of Robinson Financial Services. Robinson provides a variety of services ranging from financial advice to estate planning and 401K plan administration. Recently, Robinson began selling a package of financial planning tools that includes books, planning documents, and a DVD video. This package is marketed and sold through Robinson's online store. Unfortunately, the customer service staff at Robinson has been unable to contact several of the customers who purchased the package. Linda Adams has decided to send personalized letters to all customers thanking them for their purchases and requesting that they provide Robinson with valid phone numbers.

Introducing Mail Merge

Word's Mail Merge feature is most often used for generating personalized form letters, mailing labels, and envelopes. However, Mail Merge is a versatile tool that can be used with any type of document. Mail Merge can be a big time-saver and is invaluable for managing large mailings.

Components of a Mail Merge

Merging creates a merge document by combining information from two or more documents. The documents are known as the *main document* and the *data source*.

- **Main Document**—This document controls the merge. It contains the fixed information into which the variable information for each contact is merged. An example of a typical merge document is a standard form letter.

- **Data Source**—This can be another Word document, a spreadsheet, a database file, or a contacts list in Outlook.

You can merge an existing main document with an existing data source, or you can create the main document and data source while stepping through the merge process.

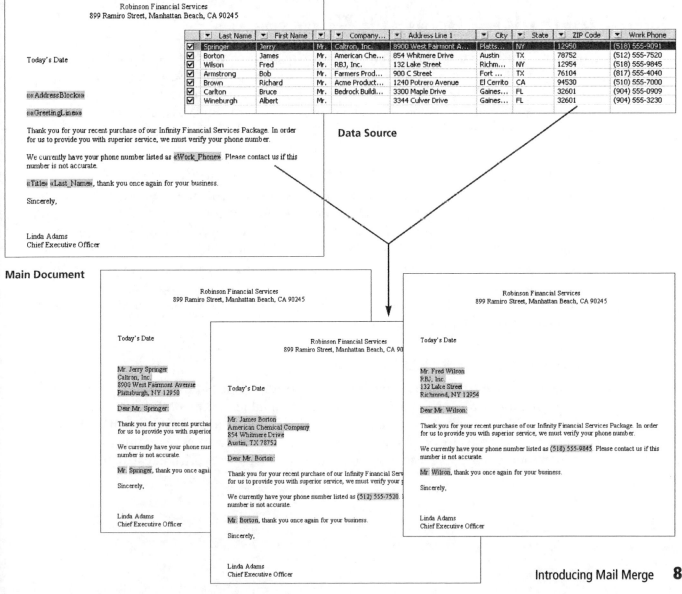

Data Source

Main Document

The Benefits of Using Mail Merge

Mail Merge will save you a lot of time and can help reduce errors in large mailings. You will really appreciate Mail Merge when you produce form letters and then later decide you want to make a change. Using Mail Merge, you can edit the main document once and remerge it with the data source to produce a new merge document. Without Mail Merge, you would need to edit each personalized letter individually.

The Mailings Tab

The Mailings tab on the Ribbon provides guidance in setting up both the main document and data source and helps you conduct the merge. The Start Mail Merge command group on the Mailings tab is the beginning point.

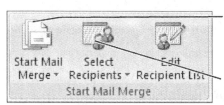

The Start Mail Merge command is where you specify the type of main document you want to use, such as letters, envelopes, or labels.

Select Recipients is where you either identify an existing data source list or create a new data source.

Working with the Data Source

Data sources usually contain names, addresses, telephone numbers, and other contact information. However, you can include any information in a data source. For example, you may want to include inventory names, numbers, and prices of parts, if you are using Mail Merge to create a parts catalog. You can create a data source in Word, or you can use external data sources, such as an Access database or an Excel worksheet.

Designing Effective Data Sources

It is very important that you design effective data sources. The most important consideration is the number of fields to use. The more fields, the more flexibility you will have in the merge. An important rule to remember is that you cannot merge a portion of a field. For example, if a field contains both a first name and last name, then you will never be able to merge only the last name into a main document. This would be a problem if you needed to merge only a last name to create salutations such as Dear Ms. Alvarez. In this example, you would need to use one field for the first name and a separate field for the last name. You would also need to use a title field for the titles Mr., Ms., and Mrs.

Creating Address Lists

You use the New Address List dialog box to set up address lists (data sources) for use in mail merges. This tool stores the addresses you enter in a table within a Microsoft Access database. This table, which becomes the data source for the merge, is linked to the mail merge main document. You can use a Word table, an Excel worksheet, or an Access table as a data source for a mail merge. Each of these tools stores data in a table or worksheet structure.

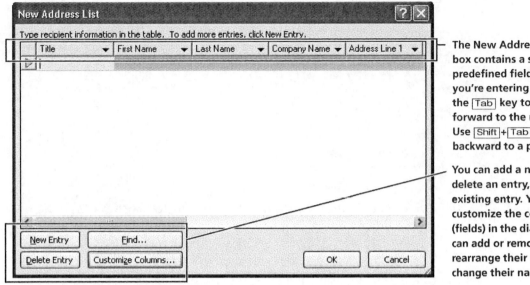

The New Address List dialog box contains a set of predefined fields. When you're entering data, you use the `Tab` key to move forward to the next field. Use `Shift`+`Tab` to move backward to a previous field.

You can add a new entry, delete an entry, or find an existing entry. You can also customize the columns (fields) in the dialog box; you can add or remove fields, rearrange their order, or change their names.

Customizing an Address List

The Customize Address List dialog box makes it easy to set up the mailing list just as you want it. You can easily delete unnecessary fields and add your own custom fields to the list.

Choose the field you want to delete.

Click the Delete button.

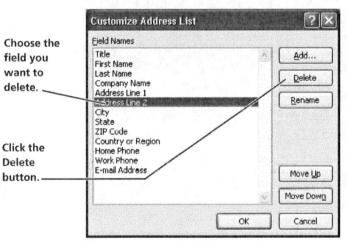

Delete a field from the list.

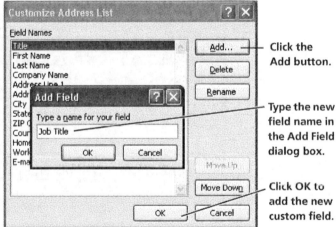

Click the Add button.

Type the new field name in the Add Field dialog box.

Click OK to add the new custom field.

Add a field to the list.

 Hands-On 5.1 **Specify the Main Document and Create a Data Source**

1. Start Word. Make sure the Word window is maximized 🗖.

2. If necessary, start a new document.

3. Choose Mailings→Start Mail Merge→Start Mail Merge 📄 from the Ribbon.

4. Choose Letters from the menu, as shown at right.

5. Choose Mailings→Start Mail Merge→Select Recipients 📇 from the Ribbon.

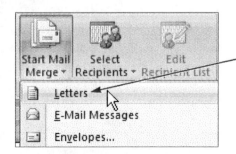

6. Choose Type New List from the menu.

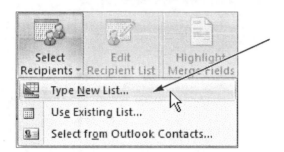

7. Click the Customize Columns button in the bottom-left corner of the dialog box to display the Customize Address List dialog box.

8. Choose the Address Line 2 field.

9. Click the Delete button, and then click Yes when the message appears to verify the deletion.

10. Delete the Country or Region, Home Phone, and E-mail Address fields.

11. Click OK to complete the changes.

12. Position the cursor in the Title field (if necessary), type **Ms.**, and then tap Tab to move to the next field.

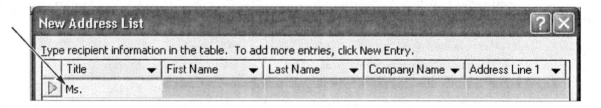

13. Type **Isabel**, and then tap Tab to move to the next field.

14. Type **Alvarez**, and then tap Tab to move to the next field.

15. Finish entering the Isabel Alvarez data shown in the following table, tabbing between fields. The list of fields will scroll as you continue to Tab and type.

16. When you complete the first record, click the New Entry button or tap Tab to generate a new blank row for the next record, and then enter the two remaining records shown in the following table.

Ms. Isabel Alvarez	Mr. Peter Zantos	Mr. John Hemmet
American Chemical Company	RBJ, Inc.	Farmers Products
854 Whitmere Drive	132 Lake Street	900 C Street
Austin TX 78752	Richmond NY 12954	Fort Worth TX 76104
512-555-7520	518-555-9845	817-555-4040

17. Leave the New Address List dialog box open, and you will review your entries in the next exercise.

Reviewing Your Records

It's a good idea to review your records for accuracy before saving the data source. However, if you miss an error, you can always edit it in the Edit Data Source dialog box, which you'll learn about later in this lesson.

If an entry is wider than the default field width, you can click the cursor directly in the field and use the arrow keys to move through the entry.

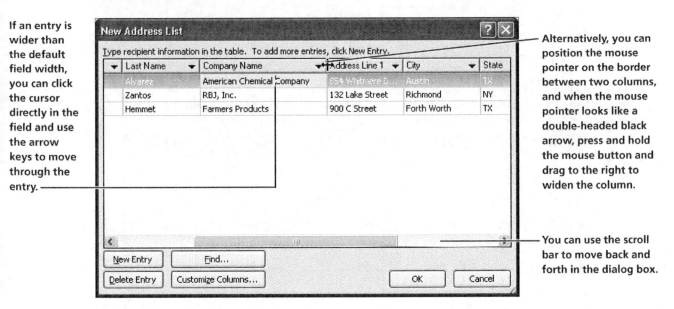

Alternatively, you can position the mouse pointer on the border between two columns, and when the mouse pointer looks like a double-headed black arrow, press and hold the mouse button and drag to the right to widen the column.

You can use the scroll bar to move back and forth in the dialog box.

 Hands-On 5.2   Review and Save Your Work

1. Position the mouse pointer on the scroll bar and drag left and right to view all the fields.

2. Click the cursor in the Company Name field for the first record, and use the arrow keys on the keyboard to move the cursor through the entry.

3. Position the mouse pointer on the border between the Company Name and Address Line 1 fields, and when the mouse pointer changes to a double-headed black arrow, drag to the right to display the entire American Chemical Company entry.

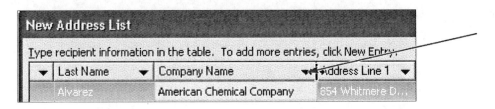

4. Make any needed revisions.

5. When you finish reviewing your records, click OK to open the Save Address List dialog box.

6. Save the data as **Merge Data** in the Lesson 05 folder.

7. Leave the current document open, and stay in the Mailings tab on the Ribbon for the next exercise.

Managing the Address List

The Mail Merge Recipients dialog box lets you sort and filter address lists and choose records to include in a mail merge. To edit data, you click the Edit button in the Mail Merge Recipients dialog box to display the Edit Data Source dialog box, where you can add, delete, and edit entries.

You choose→Mailings→Start Mail Merge→Edit Recipient List ⬛ from the Ribbon to access the Mail Merge Recipients dialog box.

If there are records that you do not want to include in your mailing, use the menu▼ buttons to display a filter list allowing you to temporarily hide records based on filter criteria.

You can sort the list based on any field by clicking the desired field heading.

Only records that are checked are used in the mail merge. Individual records can be checked or unchecked by clicking their checkboxes. All records can be checked or unchecked at once using the checkbox at the top of the column.

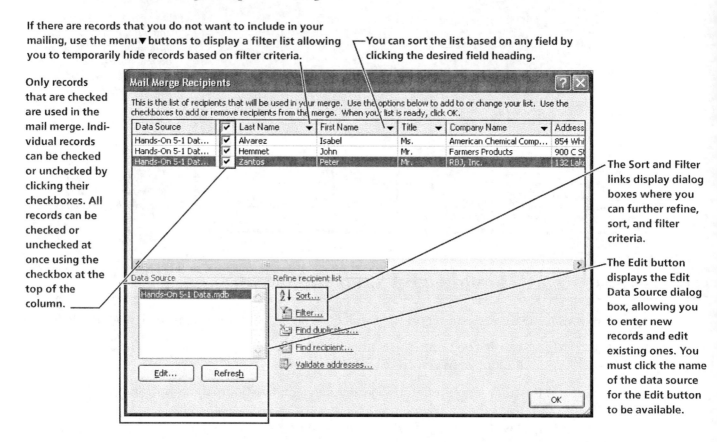

The Sort and Filter links display dialog boxes where you can further refine, sort, and filter criteria.

The Edit button displays the Edit Data Source dialog box, allowing you to enter new records and edit existing ones. You must click the name of the data source for the Edit button to be available.

The Edit Data Source dialog box looks and operates like the New Address List dialog box that you used to enter the original list.

Hands-On 5.3 **Use Mail Merge Recipient Options and Edit Records**

1. Choose→Mailings→Start Mail Merge→Edit Recipient List 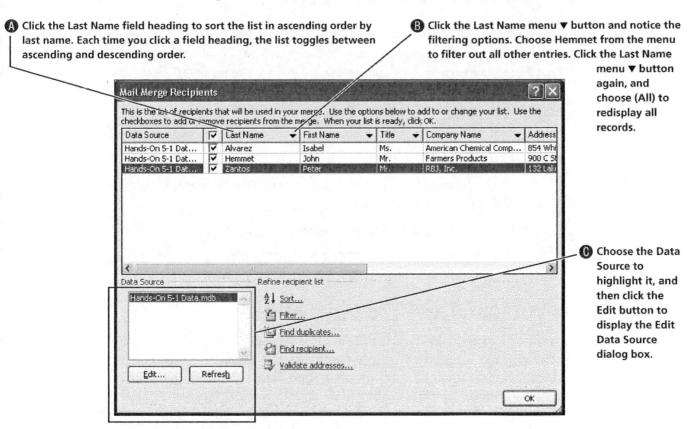 from the Ribbon.

2. Follow these steps to sort and filter the list and open the Edit Data Source dialog box:

A Click the Last Name field heading to sort the list in ascending order by last name. Each time you click a field heading, the list toggles between ascending and descending order.

B Click the Last Name menu ▼ button and notice the filtering options. Choose Hemmet from the menu to filter out all other entries. Click the Last Name menu ▼ button again, and choose (All) to redisplay all records.

C Choose the Data Source to highlight it, and then click the Edit button to display the Edit Data Source dialog box.

3. Click the *Farmers Products* field to highlight the text.

4. Type **Miners Products Company** in its place.

5. Follow these guidelines to enter the following three records:

- Use the New Entry button or tap [Tab] for each new record.
- Tap [Tab] to move from one field to the next.
- Notice that the third record does not include a company name. Tap [Tab] to pass through the Company Name field and leave it empty.
- Make sure to enter the data in the correct fields.

Mr. Stanley Zarnett	Mr. Bruce Carlton	Ms. Ella Lew
Acme Products, Inc.	Bedrock Building Supplies	3344 Culver Drive
1240 Potrero Avenue	3300 Maple Drive	Gainesville FL 32601
El Cerrito CA 94530	Gainesville FL 32601	904-555-3230
510-555-7000	904-555-0909	

6. Click OK to close the dialog box.

7. Click Yes when the message appears verifying your update, and then notice your changes in the Mail Merge Recipients dialog box.

8. Click OK to close the Mail Merge Recipients dialog box.

Working with Main Documents

You accomplish a merge by combining a main document with a data source. Typical main documents include form letters, envelopes, and mailing labels. A main document is linked to a data source that includes one or more merge fields. Merge fields inserted into a main document correspond to fields in the attached data source. Some merge fields, such as the address block, are composite fields consisting of a number of fields grouped together. For example, Title, First Name, and Last Name would be included in the address block merge field.

When you conduct a merge, a customized letter, envelope, or label is created for each record in the data source. The following figure shows the command buttons in the Write & Insert Fields group of the Mailings tab that you will use to insert merge fields into your letter.

This command allows you to insert an address block for an inside address in your letter.

This command lets you insert a greeting line.

Use this button to insert any of the fields from your data source.

The following illustration shows the form letter you will set up and the various merge fields it will contain.

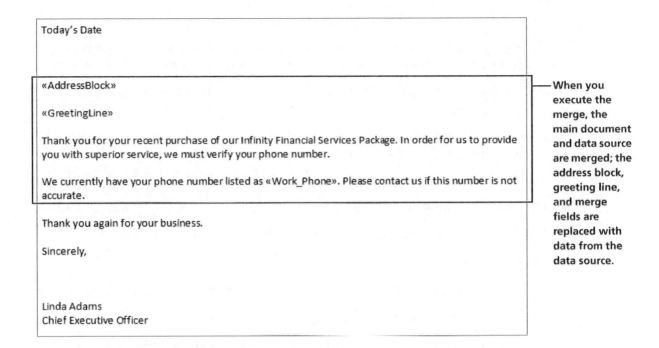

Today's Date

«AddressBlock»

«GreetingLine»

Thank you for your recent purchase of our Infinity Financial Services Package. In order for us to provide you with superior service, we must verify your phone number.

We currently have your phone number listed as «Work_Phone». Please contact us if this number is not accurate.

Thank you again for your business.

Sincerely,

Linda Adams
Chief Executive Officer

When you execute the merge, the main document and data source are merged; the address block, greeting line, and merge fields are replaced with data from the data source.

Setting Up Main Documents

You can use any document as a mail merge main document. A document becomes a main document when you attach it to a data source and insert merge fields. In this lesson, you create a main document from the blank document you started in the first exercise. However, you can open any document and use it as a main document by using the Select Recipients command in the Start Mail Merge group on the Ribbon to attach a data source. Once a data source is attached, you can insert merge fields.

 Hands-On 5.4   Set Up a Form Letter

1. If necessary, choose Home→Paragraph→Show/Hide ¶ from the Ribbon to display formatting characters.

2. Select the paragraph symbol.

3. Choose Home→Paragraph→Line Spacing from the Ribbon.

4. Choose 1.0 line spacing, and then click the Line Spacing button again and choose Remove Space After Paragraph.

5. Type the following text, and then select and center align it.

> Robinson Financial Services
> 899 Ramiro Street, Manhattan Beach, CA 90245

6. Position the cursor at the end of the address line, tap Enter and choose Home→Paragraph Align Text Left from the Ribbon.

7. If necessary, click the View Ruler ⊠ button at the top of the scroll bar to display the ruler.

8. Tap [Enter] enough times after the address to position the cursor approximately 2 inches from the top of the page, which is the 1-inch mark on the vertical ruler.

9. Choose Insert→Text→Insert Date and Time 🔢 from the Ribbon to display the Date and Time dialog box.

10. Choose the third date format on the list, check the Update Automatically checkbox in the bottom-right corner of the dialog box, and then click OK.

11. Tap [Enter] four times after inserting the date.

12. Choose Mailings→Write & Insert Fields→Address Block 📄 from the Ribbon.

13. If necessary, choose the Mr. Joshua Randall Jr. option, and click OK.

14. Tap [Enter] twice.

15. Choose Mailings→Write & Insert Fields→Greeting Line 📄 from the Ribbon.

16. Follow these steps to modify and insert the greeting line:

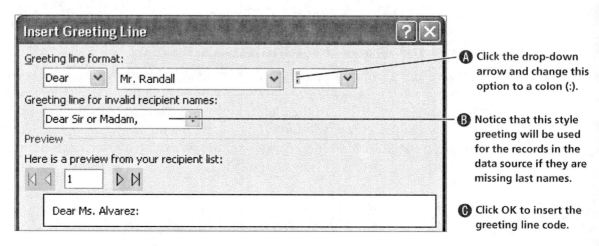

Ⓐ Click the drop-down arrow and change this option to a colon (:).

Ⓑ Notice that this style greeting will be used for the records in the data source if they are missing last names.

Ⓒ Click OK to insert the greeting line code.

17. Tap [Enter] twice, and then type the first and second paragraphs shown in the letter at the end of this exercise, until you reach the location that requires the Work_Phone field. Continue with step 18 when you get to that point.

18. Choose Mailings→Write & Insert Fields→Insert Merge Fields 📇 from the Ribbon.

19. Choose the Work Phone field, and click the Insert button.

20. Click the Close button to close the Insert Merge Field dialog box.

21. Type a period, and then type the remainder of the letter.

> Robinson Financial Services
> 899 Ramiro Street, Manhattan Beach, CA 90245
>
> Today's Date
>
>
> «AddressBlock»
>
> «GreetingLine»
>
> Thank you for your recent purchase of our Infinity Financial Services Package. In order for us to provide you with superior service, we must verify your phone number.
>
> We currently have your phone number listed as «Work_Phone». Please contact us if this number is not accurate.
>
> Thank you again for your business.
>
> Sincerely,
>
>
> Linda Adams
> Chief Executive Officer

22. Take a few moments to review your letter, making sure it matches the preceding example. In particular, make sure you used the proper punctuation and spacing between fields and the text. Any punctuation or spacing errors that occur in your form letter will appear in every merged letter.

23. Save 💾 the letter in the Lesson 05 folder as **Merge Main**.

Conducting a Merge

Merging combines a main document with a data source to produce a merge document. If you are merging a form letter with a data source, Word produces a personalized copy of the form letter for each record in the data source.

Previewing the Results

The Preview Results group on the Mailings tab allows you to see how your letters will look before you complete the merge.

You can click the Preview Results button to display the first record from your data source in the letter.

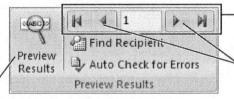

The navigate button lets you browse through the merge letters. There is one letter for each record in the data source. The far left and right arrows take you to the first and last records in the list.

These arrows move back and forth through the list, one record at a time.

Finishing the Merge

When you feel confident that your letter and data source are accurate, you use the Finish & Merge command.

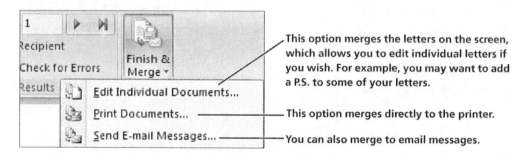

This option merges the letters on the screen, which allows you to edit individual letters if you wish. For example, you may want to add a P.S. to some of your letters.

This option merges directly to the printer.

You can also merge to email messages.

To Save or Not to Save

Merge documents are rarely saved, because they can easily be reconstructed by merging the main document with the data source. A merge document is usually previewed, printed, and closed without saving. If a merge document contains errors, you can close it without saving, edit the main document or data source, and then conduct the merge again.

 Hands-On 5.5 **Conduct the Merge**

1. Choose Mailings→Preview Results→Preview Results [icon] from the Ribbon to view the data from the first record.

2. Use the navigation buttons in the Preview Results group to scroll through all your merged documents.

3. Choose Mailings→Finish→Finish & Merge [icon] from the Ribbon.

4. Choose Edit Individual Documents from the menu to merge the letters on the screen.

5. Click OK to merge all records.

6. Scroll through the letters and scan their contents.

7. Leave the merge document open to use in the next exercise.

Working with Merge Problems

Several common errors can cause a merge to produce incorrect results. The merge document (or preview) will usually provide clues as to why a merge fails to produce the intended results. Once you identify an error in the merge document, you can make changes to the main document or the data source. You can then conduct the merge again to determine if the error was fixed. Repeat this process until the merge works as intended.

 Hands-On 5.6   **Fix Merge Problems**

1. Browse through the merge document and look for any errors. Note any errors in a separate Word document or on a piece of paper. Indicate how often the errors occur (in every merged letter or just one).

2. If you find an error that occurs in *every merged letter,* close the merge document without saving and edit the main document, and then save it.

3. If you find a data error in *just one letter,* close the merge document without saving it.

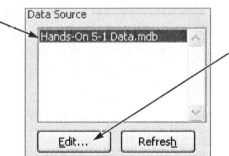

- Choose Mailings→Start Mail Merge→Edit Recipient List 🗹 from the Ribbon.

- When the Mail Merge Recipients dialog box appears, highlight the Data Source in the bottom-left corner of the dialog box, and click the Edit button.

- After you fix any errors, click OK, and then click Yes when the message appears asking if you want to update the data.

- Click OK to close the Mail Merge Recipients dialog box.

4. When you have corrected any errors, execute the merge again.

5. Close the merge document without saving it.

6. Save and close Merge Main.

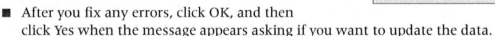

Using Envelopes and Labels with Mail Merge

When you choose Mailings→Start Mail Merge→Start Mail Merge 📄 from the Ribbon, Word presents you with options for the type of main document you want to create. In addition to form letters, you can use envelopes, labels, and other types of documents as main documents.

You can use the same data source for various main documents. For example, you can use the same data source for envelopes and mailing labels that you used for the form letter.

Generating Envelopes with Mail Merge

You can use Mail Merge to generate an envelope for each record in a data source. Mail Merge lets you choose the envelope size and formats.

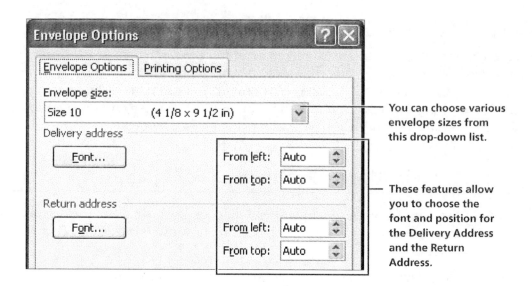

You can choose various envelope sizes from this drop-down list.

These features allow you to choose the font and position for the Delivery Address and the Return Address.

 Hands-On 5.7 **Choose an Envelope Size and Attach a Data Source**

1. Start a new blank document.

2. Choose Mailings→Start Mail Merge→Start Mail Merge ⬚ from the Ribbon, and then choose Envelopes from the menu.

3. When the Envelope Options dialog box appears, if necessary, choose Size 10 from the Envelope Size list.

4. Click OK to apply the settings to the document.

5. Choose Mailings→Start Mail Merge→Select Recipients ⬚ from the Ribbon, and then choose Use Existing List from the menu.

6. When the Select Data Source dialog box appears, navigate to your file storage location and open Merge Data from the Lesson 05 folder.

7. Stay in the Mailings tab for the next topic.

Arranging the Envelope

You can insert an address block in the envelope main document. An envelope main document can be saved like any other main document, allowing you to use it over and over to generate envelopes from a data source. The following illustration shows the envelope main document that you will set up in the next exercise.

The return address is typed in the top-left corner of the envelope main document.

The envelope has a rectangular placeholder for the address block. You must click the placeholder before inserting the address block.

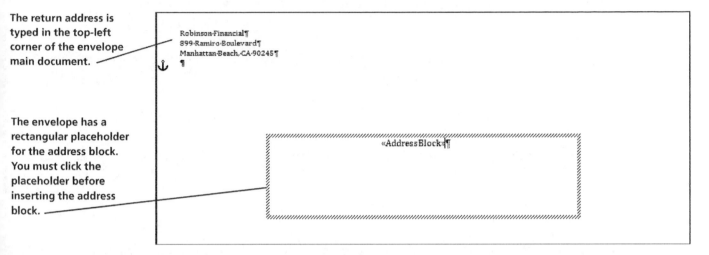

 Hands-On 5.8   Merge to Envelopes

1. Type the return address, starting at the first paragraph symbol in the upper-left corner of the envelope, as shown here.

   Robinson·Financial¶
   899·Ramiro·Boulevard¶
   Manhattan·Beach,·CA·90245¶
   ¶

2. Click the I-beam toward the center bottom half of the envelope, to display the address block placeholder.

3. Choose Mailings→Write & Insert Fields→Address Block from the Ribbon.

4. Click OK to accept the default address block settings.

5. Choose Mailings→Preview Results→Preview Results from the Ribbon to display the first record from the data source in the envelope.

6. Use the navigation buttons in the Preview Results group to scroll through all your merged envelopes.

7. Choose Mailings→Finish→Finish & Merge from the Ribbon.

8. Choose Edit Individual Documents from the menu, and then click OK to merge all the records.

9. Scroll through the envelopes, and notice that there is one envelope for each record in the data source.

10. If necessary, fix any problems with the mail merge.

11. When you finish, close the merge document without saving it.

12. Turn off the Preview Results button, and then save the envelope in the Lesson 05 folder as **Merge Envelope** and close it.

Generating Labels with Mail Merge

You can use Mail Merge to generate mailing labels for each record in a data source. Mail Merge lets you choose the label format, sheet size, and other specifications. It also lets you insert an address block and other fields in the main document. Like other main documents, a labels main document can be saved for future use. The following illustration shows a portion of the labels main document that you will set up in the next exercise.

Using Label Options

The Label Options dialog box allows you to choose printer options and the type of label you will use for your merge.

Choose the appropriate printer information in this area.

Choose the product brand from this drop-down list.

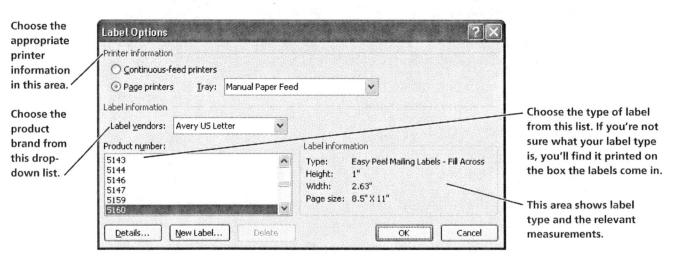

Choose the type of label from this list. If you're not sure what your label type is, you'll find it printed on the box the labels come in.

This area shows label type and the relevant measurements.

1. Start a new blank document.

2. If necessary, choose Home→Paragraph→Show/Hide ¶ from the Ribbon to display formatting marks.

3. Choose Mailings→Start Mail Merge → Start Mail Merge from the Ribbon, and then choose Labels from the menu.

4. When the Label Options dialog box appears, if necessary, choose Avery US Letter from the Label Vendors drop-down list, and then choose 5160 from the Product Number list.

5. Click OK to apply the settings to the document.

6. Choose Mailings→Start Mail Merge→Select Recipients from the Ribbon, and then choose Use Existing List from the menu.

7. When the Select Data Source dialog box opens, navigate to your file storage location and open Merge Data. Make sure the cursor is in the first address label position.

8. Choose Mailings→Write & Insert Fields→Address Block from the Ribbon.

9. Click OK to insert the address block code in the first label.

10. Choose Mailings→Write & Insert Fields→Update Labels from the Ribbon to place the address block in all of the labels.

11. Press Ctrl + A to select the entire document.

12. Choose Home→Styles from the Ribbon.

13. Choose the No Spacing style from the Quick Styles gallery.

14. Choose Mailings→Preview Results→Preview Results from the Ribbon to see how the labels will look when you print them, and then turn off the Preview Results command.

15. Choose Mailings→Finish→Finish & Merge from the Ribbon.

16. Choose Edit Individual Documents from the menu.

17. When the Merge to New Document dialog box appears, click OK to merge all the records.

18. Close your merged document without saving it.

19. Save the labels main document in the Lesson 05 folder as **Merge Labels**, and then close it.

Concepts Review

True/False Questions

1. Each row in a data source table contains one record. TRUE FALSE

2. You cannot merge a portion of a field into a main document. TRUE FALSE

3. Combining the first and last name in the same field limits the flexibility of your data source. TRUE FALSE

4. Typical form letters contain text and merge fields. TRUE FALSE

5. The merge document is usually saved. TRUE FALSE

6. Before conducting a merge, you must connect the data source to the main document. TRUE FALSE

7. You can use Mail Merge to generate mailing labels. TRUE FALSE

8. A mistake in one merged letter indicates an error in the main document. TRUE FALSE

9. You can use the Mail Merge Recipients dialog box to sort and filter records in a data source. TRUE FALSE

10. When you use the New Address List dialog box to set up a mailing list, Word stores the addresses you enter in a Microsoft Excel file. TRUE FALSE

Multiple Choice Questions

1. Which of the following tasks can you accomplish in the Mail Merge Recipients dialog box?
   a. Delete a record.
   b. Sort the list.
   c. Add a record.
   d. Execute the merge.

2. To qualify as a main document, a letter must _____.
   a. use a sorted data source
   b. include merge fields
   c. use Word 2007's default line and paragraph spacing
   d. contain records

3. Which of the following can you use as a mail merge main document?
   a. An Excel workbook
   b. A Word letter
   c. An Access database
   d. All of the above

4. Which of the following is accurate regarding mail merge labels?
   a. You must have a page of labels in the printer before executing the merge.
   b. You cannot insert merge fields in a labels document.
   c. You cannot save a labels main document for future use.
   d. You can use the same data source you used to create a mail merge letter.

Index

ITEM: 1-59136-200-8
ISBN-13: 978-1-59136-200-5

9 781591 362005